ON THE EDGE

ON THE EDGE

Recent Perspectives on Police Suicide

By

JOHN M. VIOLANTI

Social and Preventative Medicine
School of Public Health and Health Professions
State University of New York
Buffalo, New York

ANDREW F. O'HARA

Executive Director
Badge of Life
Psychological Survival for Police Officers

TERESA T. TATE

Founder, Survivors of Law Enforcement Suicide (SOLES)

CHARLES C THOMAS • PUBLISHER, LTD.
Springfield • Illinois • U.S.A.

Published and Distributed Throughout the World by

CHARLES C THOMAS • PUBLISHER, LTD.
2600 South First Street
Springfield, Illinois 62704

ISBN 978-0-398-08632-9 (hard)
ISBN 978-0-398-08633-6 (paper)
ISBN 978-0-398-08634-3 (ebook)

Library of Congress Catalog Card Number: 2010042334

With THOMAS BOOKS *careful attention is given to all details of manufacturing and design. It is the Publisher's desire to present books that are satisfactory as to their physical qualities and artistic possibilities and appropriate for their particular use.* THOMAS BOOKS *will be true to those laws of quality that assure a good name and good will.*

Printed in the United States of America
SM-R-3

Library of Congress Cataloging-in-Publication Data

Violanti, John M.
On the edge : recent perspectives on police suicide / by John M. Violanti, Andrew F. O'Hara, Teresa T. Tate.
p. cm.
Includes bibliographical references and index.
ISBN 978-0-398-08632-9 (hard) -- ISBN 978-0-398-08633-6 (pbk.) -- ISBN 978-0-398-08634-3 (ebook)
1. Police--Suicidal behavior--United States. 2. Police--Job stress--United States. 3. Suicide--United States--Prevention. I. O'Hara, Andrew F. II. Tate, Teresa T. III. Title.

HV7936.S77V558 2011
362.28088'3632--dc22

2010042334

To those police officers who have left us
To those who were left behind

PREFACE

I watched my husband deteriorate the last three to four weeks of his life, and I couldn't stop it. He shot and killed himself the morning of March 8, 1995, in an undercover facility where we had lived in isolation and anonymity for the last year of his life. He was 45 years old. I wanted so desperately to have someone come over and try to talk with him, to help us, but no one could visit the house or know where we lived or what we did; not even other agents or family. There was nowhere to turn. I felt helpless and hopeless. Pacing . . . wringing hands. . . . I can't do it. . . . I begged him – let's just walk out the door and leave. . . . Take nothing with us, just get in the car and go. We lived in a fishbowl, you see; it was the only way; but, he would not even consider it. Being an FBI Agent was who he was, how he defined himself.

He was like many of you – driven personality, unable to show his emotions, he had to appear unshakable, strong, and independent. He was my rock. With cops, there's always a wall, even with family members, even when we were both cops. In other words, he had to be no less than perfect. These are admirable qualities in a person and desirable qualities we want in our law enforcement. We want strong, motivated, and independent personnel who can take charge of any given situation. However, these qualities come with a price. We must change the perception in our law enforcement institutions that you "suck it up and go on." We need to be there for our own. Certainly, no one else will be.

Donna Shulz, Police Suicide Survivor

Donna's comments give a first-hand personal view of the tragedy and hopelessness associated with police suicide. FBI Agent Bruce Shulz was a good man, a good husband, and a good cop. His death brings to mind the sometimes devastating psychological impact of police work on those who choose to serve.

The multi-dimensional character of suicide makes it extremely difficult to focus on specific attributes of the police occupation which exacerbate suicide. First and foremost is the violent nature of the work and accouterments associated with protection from that violence. Police work inherently involves violence and death. The human psyche of police officers must be continuously battered by the stress and trauma of this violence experience. In all probability, multifaceted stress and trauma experienced over the length of a police career can take its psychological toll. Additionally, the aftermath of a police suicide leaves survivors who are at times forgotten or isolated from an agency that was once the "police family."

In our previous books on police suicide, we enumerated academic research in an attempt to help clarify this tragic problem. In the present book, we plan to extend that research to a national level. Also noticeably absent from previous work were the untold story of those officers who have experienced the context of suicide. We hope that the addition of Andrew O'Hara, and Teresa Tate as authors will add a realistic description of what it is like to be "on the edge." Andy, a former police officer, survived his near suicide and now describes the feelings and pain he felt during that crisis period. Teresa survived the death of her spouse, a police officer who died by suicide. The insight that Andy and Teresa bring to this writing will add immeasurably to our understanding of this problem.

This book will consist of the following areas of discussion (1) a description of the police suicide rate research; (2) a conceptual model of the life course trauma and police officers with possible relationships to suicide potential; (3) a discussion of resiliency and police personal and organizational factors which contribute to psychological protection against suicide; (4) the reality of individual suicide – a qualitative detailed description of an officer's encounter with suicide; (5) the plight of police suicide survivors; and (6) approaches to suicide prevention.

In Chapter 1, our discussion centers on police suicide rates and the ongoing controversy that surrounds this area of research. In Chapter 2, we describe two in-depth analyses of *national* police suicide rates. The first was based on the Centers for Disease Control (CDC) National Occupational Mortality Surveillance (NOMS) database. The National Institute for Occupational Safety and Health (NIOSH) maintains the NOMS System database of death certificate data with standard coded occupation and industry information. Twenty-eight states have participated in the project. The second source of national data was obtained from a two year-long web surveillance of police suicide media reports. This strategy was found to provide the most reliable return of near real-time media information from radio, television and press, both local and national. Approximately 119,000 suicide-specific news articles were reviewed during the year for information relating to police suicides in the United States. Results of these informative national explorations will be discussed in this chapter.

Chapter 3 is based on a conceptual model of the career span of a police officer and trauma within that span which may exacerbate conditions for suicide. We will borrow from life course theory to develop this model. The average career length of a police officer in the United States is approximately 20–25 years. During this time, serving officers face the prospect of repeated exposure to death, human misery, and the worse of society. Most of the research, however, has focused on the consequences of specific events that are located at a single point in an officer's career. While informative, such brief snapshots can provide only limited insights into a reality that will extend over decades.

Chapter 4 presents a discussion of factors which may help to *protect* police officers from suicide. Here we develop ideas about salutogenic approaches to suicide and how officers may grow from trauma exposure instead of being devastated by it. The ability to be resilient, to "bounce back" from traumatic experiences, is an important factor in police officer psychological survival. In this respect, not only police officers but also organizations and leaders have a number of responsibilities to their officers in the enhancement of resilience. The police organization has a responsibility to develop policies, procedures and practices designed, as far as possible, to facilitate officer's ability maintain a sense of coherence between organizational expectations and occupational experiences, thereby minimizing the occurrence and impact of chronic stress. The impact of organizational factors at all levels of occupational experience illustrates the potential for management to instill preventative mechanisms in employees at each of these levels – neglect at any level will increase employee vulnerability and the potential for suicide.

In Chapter 5, we bring home the qualitative nature of police suicide. Here we see the reality of police suicide on an *individual level* described from the viewpoint of Andy O'Hara, an officer who was "on the edge" and back. As we continue to explore police suicide theories, rates, and causes, we sometimes forget the individual nature of suicide and how such decisions may come about in police officers. Andy lucidly describes his own journey to the edge.

In Chapter 6, Andy O'Hara presents a description of innovative approaches to police suicide prevention. In his newly developed program called the "Badge of Life," O'Hara seeks to "depower" police trauma and, instead, "empower" the officer. By empowerment, we mean giving each officer the simple tools they need for self-care, by which they can approach their work with a clear awareness of their emotional strengths and their ability to make wise choices. In doing so, they will be prepared not only for stress, but for trauma before it occurs and know what to do when it does. The two primary tools he proposes are as simple as they are universal. Such ideas as "annual mental health checkups" and conceptualizations about "balanced reality" by which police recruits at the academy level can prepare themselves for a wider range of experience than that generally afforded in the regimented academy experience. In addition to the development of new ideas,

O'Hara discusses strategies in selecting a mental health professional who understand police work.

In Chapter 7, we move to the after-effects of police suicide. Many persons suffer from suicide. Nationwide, there are six survivors for every suicide. Survivors face considerable difficulties due to the violent nature of firearm suicide, guilt, and mourning rituals such as police funerals. It is likely that suicide is viewed as an unheroic death in the police milieu, and survivors must deal with their own grief as well as negative reactions of police peers, the police organization, and the public. Quite often, survivors of police suicide are abandoned more quickly than those of officers who died from other causes due to the stigma associated with such deaths. A recently completed study by this author found that police support can help to ameliorate psychological distress and trauma associated with an officer's death. A forgotten layer of survivors also exists within the department itself. Peer officers, supervisors, and support personnel are all subject to grief responses when a coworker commits suicide.

In this chapter, Teresa Tate, founder and leader of the survivor group S.O.L.E.S. (Survivors of Law Enforcement Suicide) presents actual cases of police survivors derived from her personal interviews with these survivors. Ms. Tate also suggests policy revisions for police to help survivors through the aftermath of suicide. Based on these cases, police departments can profit from the mistakes of the past that have occurred to survivors over the years. Law enforcement leaders should be able to show compassion and sensitivity to the families so as not to add to their pain.

In the final chapter, we conclude with a description and critical analysis of present programs for police suicide prevention. We ask the question "what next?" and discuss the need for more comprehensive prevention research. Contributions in this book can be useful to law enforcement practitioners as well as researchers and therapists. Certainly areas of police organizational policy can benefit from our discussions. We hope that offerings put forth here will spur new ideas to assist persons who work in this difficult, unforgiving, and psychologically dangerous occupation.

CONTENTS

ON THE EDGE

Chapter 1

THE CONTROVERSY OF POLICE SUICIDE RATES

JOHN M. VIOLANTI

There are many estimates of police suicide rates throughout the academic literature. Some of the sources of these estimates are empirical, some lack scientific rigor, and some appear to be anecdotal. Because of the lack of measurable data and information on police suicides, it remains difficult to pin down an exact number. This issue has raised considerable controversy as to whether or not police suicides are higher than those of the general population. There are those who say "why bother" and that the important thing is to prevent police suicide. I agree with this conjecture, but I still see the necessity of gathering an accurate assessment of the magnitude of the problem. It is through this that police organizations and policy makers can be convinced that we indeed do need prevention programs.

ARE POLICE SUICIDE RATES HIGHER? DISAGREEMENT

Kappeler, Blumberg, and Potter (1993) argued that the connection between police stress and suicide is a myth that perpetuates public perception of "battered and blue crime-fighters." Other researchers have attributed police suicide more to the facts that (1) the police occupation is male dominated and statistically males commit suicide more often than do females, and (2) officers have a readily available lethal method with which to commit suicide (Alpert & Dunham, 1988).

Aamodt and Stalnaker (2001) suggested that, although the suicide rate of 18.1/100,000 for law enforcement personnel is higher than the rate of 11.4/100,000 in the general population, it is not higher than would be expected for people of similar age, race, and gender. Thus any difference between law enforcement rates and rates in the general population can be adequately explained by the race, gender, and age of people who enter the law enforcement field. This is an important point because it suggests that such factors as job stress and the availability of weapons are not factors that are exclusively associated with law enforcement suicide. The authors conclude that allocating mental health resources to law enforcement personnel at the expense of other professions does not appear justified. Furthermore, the reasons that officers commit suicide are similar to those of the general population, with the possible exception of legal problems.

Hem, Berg, and Ekeberg (2001) published a systematic critical review of suicide among police. They identified forty-one original studies from North America, Europe, and Australia. The results indicated that some studies found elevated suicide rates among police officers; others showed an average or low rate of suicide. However, the rates varied widely and were inconsistent and inconclusive. Most studies were conducted in limited specific police populations, where local and regional variations in suicide can affect the rates of police suicide. Moreover, the reason for studying police suicide in a specific region may be due to a suicide cluster.

Loo (2003) conducted a meta-analysis of police suicide rates and ratios using 101 samples from the literature. Large effect sizes showed that suicide rates based on short time frames were significantly higher than they were for long time frames. There were regional differences such that rates in the Americas and Europe were higher than in the Caribbean and Asian regions. There were differences in rates among federal, regional, and municipal police forces. Loo concluded that researchers need to include the use of longer time frames when studying police suicide and include controls for year of suicide, gender, ethnic groups, and rates for population comparison groups.

Marzuk, Nock, Leon, Portera, and Tardiff (2002) conducted a study of New York City police officer suicide. Marzuk and associates concluded that the suicide rates for New York City police officers were below those of the adjusted New York population. Among the 668 deaths of police officers from 1977 to 1996, 80 were certified suicides (mean age = 33.5 years). Firearms were used in 93.8 percent of these suicides; other methods included hanging, carbon monoxide poisoning, and falling from a height. The overall suicide rate among police officers during the period was 14.9 per 100,000 person-years (95% confidence interval [CI] = 11.9–18.6), compared with the demographically adjusted suicide rate for the New York City population (18.3 per 100,000 person-years, 95% CI = 18.0–18.6). The suicide rate for the upper end of the range, which included the 80 police officer suicides plus 22 additional deaths by methods usually seen in suicides, was 19.0 per 100,000 person-years (95% CI = 15.5–23.1). Marzuk and colleagues (2002) added that although the annual suicide rates varied (Figure 3–1), there were no evident trends. For seventeen of the twenty years examined, the police officer suicide rate remained below that of the demographically adjusted rate of the New York City population.

Earlier studies have also found a police suicide rate similar to or lower than the general population. Dash and Reiser (1978) found Los Angeles police officers to have a seven-year average suicide rate of 8.1/100,000 compared to a 12.6/100,00 rate nationally. A twelve-year follow-up study by Josephson and Reiser (1990) of the same department found an average suicide rate of 12/100,000 among police compared to 13.4/100,000 in Los Angeles and 14.8/100,000 in the state of California. Although police suicides were lower than other geographic rates, these authors also found that the incidence of suicide in the Los Angeles Police Department increased from 8.1/100,000 in 1976 to 12/100,000 in 1988.

Stack and Kelley (1994) completed an analysis of police suicide data from the 1985 National Mortality Detail File. Statistically controlling for age, gender, and race, these authors found the police suicide proportional mortality ratio (PMR) rate to exceed the rate of matched controls by 8 percent. This rate was not significantly higher than the rate among white males in the general population. Burnett, Boxer, and Swanson (1992) conducted a case-control study on suicide death certificate data from twenty-six states. After adjusting for age and marital and socioeconomic status, they found that police officers did have an increased risk of suicide (1.3-fold risk) over population controls but not a higher risk than other professions. Examples were pharmacists (3.3-fold risk), physicians (2.8-fold risk), lawyers (2.1-fold risk), and dentists (1.8-fold risk).

ARE POLICE SUICIDE RATES HIGHER? AGREEMENT

One would expect that the police suicide rates should be lower than they are, given that they are an employed, healthy, and psychologically tested group (McMichael, 1976). Certainly, they should be lower than the U.S. general population because this reference group includes the institutionalized, mentally ill, and unemployed.

A good amount of epidemiological evidence suggests that there is an elevated rate of suicide within law enforcement. An early national occupational study by Guralnick (1963) found the suicide ratio of male police to be 1.8 times that of the white male general population. Suicides accounted for 13.8 percent of police deaths compared to 3 percent of deaths in all other occupations, and more officers died as a result of suicide than from homicide. Milham (1979) found Washington State male police officers from 1950 to 1971 to have a suicide mortality rate higher than normally expected in the general male population.

Vena, Violanti, Marshall, and Fiedler (1986) found male officers to have an age-adjusted mortality ratio for suicide of approximately three times that of male municipal workers in the same cohort. Lester (1992) found that seven of twenty-six countries for the decade of 1980 to 1989 had police suicide rates above those of the general population. A mortality study of police officers in Rome, Italy, found the suicide ratio among male police officers to be 1.97 times as high as the general male Italian population (Forastiere et al., 1994). Violanti, Vena, and Marshall (1996) found that male police officers had a suicide rate of 8.3 times the rate of homicides and 3.1 times the rate of work accidents. Compared to male municipal workers, male police officers had a 53 percent increased rate of suicide over homicide, a threefold rate of suicide over accidents, and a 2.65-fold rate of suicide over homicide and accidents combined.

Darragh (1991) conducted an epidemiological analysis on factors based on 558 consecutive cases of self-inflicted death in the United Kingdom that revealed a dramatic increase in suicide among security force personnel. Helmkamp (1996), in a study of suicide among men in the U.S. Armed Forces, found military security and law enforcement specialists had a significantly increased rate ratio for suicide. Hartwig and Violanti (1999) found that the frequency of police suicide occurrence in Westphalia, Germany, has increased over the past seven years, particularly in the twenty-one to thirty and fifty-one to sixty age categories. Most suicides were male officers (92%). Cantor, Tyman, and Slater (1995) found the high rate of suicide among Australian police attributable to stress, health, and domestic difficulties. Occupational problems were more intense than personal ones were.

Charbonneau (2000), in a study in Quebec, Canada, found police suicide rates to be almost twice those of the general population. Rates were elevated mostly among young officers (twenty to thirty-nine years of age). Gershon, Lin, and Li (2002) provided recent evidence of job-related problems related to suicide among police officers. Officers had an approximate fourfold risk of being exposed to traumatic work events, a threefold risk of exhibiting posttraumatic stress disorder (PTSD) symptoms, a fourfold risk of alcohol abuse, and a fourfold risk of aggressive behavior.

Other factors associated with police work have been examined that could influence increased rates of suicide. Rothman and Strijdom (2002) found suicide ideation in South African police to be associated with a sense of incoherence. Officers were unable perceive traumatic police work exposures as manageable. They did not feel that they had the resources available, either personally or organizationally, to meet the demands imposed on them by their difficult work. In a nationwide study on suicide ideation and attempts among 3272 Norwegian police, Berg, Hem, Lau, Loeb, and Ekeberg (2003) found that 24 percent felt that life was not worth living, 6.4 percent seriously considered suicide, and 0.7 percent attempted suicide. Serious suicide ideation was mainly attributed to personal and family problems. Violanti (2004) found that certain traumatic police work exposures increased the risk of having a high level of PTSD symptoms, which subsequently increased the risk of alcohol use and suicide ideation. The combined impact of PTSD and increased alcohol use led to a tenfold increased risk of suicide ideation.

Depression, possibly associated with work stress and suicide ideation, may be a possible precipitant of increased police suicide risk. Violanti and his coworkers (2008) examined the association between depressive symptoms and suicide ideation in a sample of police officers. Prevalence of depression was higher among female than among male officers (12.5% verses 6.2%). For each standard deviation (SD) increase in depression symptoms, the prevalence ratio (PR) of suicide ideation increased 73 percent in female officers (PR = 1.73, 95% CI =

1.32–2.27) and 67 percent in male officers (PR = 1.67, 95% CI = 1.21–2.30).

WHAT ARE THE ISSUES?

Issues are complex in any investigation of suicide. There any many facets to consider, in both a contextual and a personal sense. Some of the issues that lead to police suicide rates are discussed in the following. This is not meant to reflect all relevant issues of police suicide; there are some that are not yet known.

Police Suicide and the Workplace

How does one define "occupational" suicide? Jenkins (2005) points out that most occupational injury fatality surveillance systems capture only incidents that occur on an employer's premises or while a worker is engaged in work activities. This does mean, however, that suicide among police officers is unrelated to their work. Suicides that are indeed driven by work-related factors may occur at the officer's home. If the stress that comes from police work is or becomes negative, it may become a risk factor (Jenkins, 2005).

What are the parameters of the police "workplace?" Johnson (1995) has commented that workplace violence does not have a uniform definition and that different kinds of violence require different insights and solutions. In addition, situational and contextual cues must be considered to define circumstances that lead to different kinds of violence. To clarify this important issue, The Association for Vital Records and Health Statistics (AVRHS), the National Institute for Occupational Safety and Health (NIOSH), the National Center for Health Statistics (NCHS), and the National Center for Environmental Health and Injury Control (NCEHIC) have jointly developed classification guidelines for what is considered "injury at work." In the category "law enforcement officer," these guidelines specifically state that any injury or fatality occurring to a police officer either *on* or *off* employer premises must be considered as a "workplace injury or death" (National Institute for Occupational Safety and Health [NIOSH], 1993, Appendix I). The reasoning behind this classification guideline is not discussed by the joint committee. It appears, however, that researchers view police work as an occupation that encompasses the life of any individual within its ranks whether on or off duty. Based on this definition, a suicide committed by a police officer away from or at the actual worksite may be considered a workplace death. It may be useful, however, to examine correlates of police suicides that occur at the actual *physical* worksite (e.g., police station) and those that occur away from that site.

"Undetermined" Death Classifications

A recent national study based on data from the Centers for Disease Control (CDC) also suggested that police deaths are classified as "undetermined" significantly more often than other first responder occupations (Violanti, in press). The results suggested that the PMR of police deaths classified as "injury undetermined whether accidentally or purposely inflicted" was significantly higher than expected in police work. Additionally, the risk of undetermined death classification nearly equaled that of suicide in the police. For male officers (PMR = 117, 95% CI = 110–123, sig $p < 0.05$) this equates to a significant 17 percent higher risk for police deaths being classified as undetermined.

Collecting Data on Police Suicide

Obtaining information on suicide from police sources is difficult. Suicide is not openly discussed by police personnel; officers tend to view suicide as dishonorable to the officer and profession (Violanti, Vena & Petralia, 1998). Departmental statistics on police suicide are rare, and police agencies are sometimes reluctant to allow researchers access to existing data. Heiman (1977) attempted to collect data on police suicide from twenty-three major U.S. cities and met with discouraging results. Even the Federal Bureau of Investigation (FBI) Uniform Crime Report (UCR) does not provide such data.

Another problem that muddles police suicide rate accuracy is the difficulty in gathering data on a national level. Countries like Finland and Sweden have national records of causes of death over many years, but such databases are not available in the United States. If one wanted to conduct a national epidemiological study on police suicide, it would take an enormous amount of resources and time. It is methodologically to verifiably collect data on every suicide in every police agency in the United States, when there are approximately 708,000 sworn officers (Reaves, 2003). Several national databases such as the National Occupational Mortality Survey (NOMS) do provide death certificate data on suicides for twenty-eight states. Future inclusion of more states and updated data may enhance knowledge on police suicide rates.

One attempt to study cross-jurisdictional police suicide rates was conducted by Langston (1995) for the National Fraternal Order of Police (FOP). Langston examined data from life insurance policy claims of 38,000 FOP members nationwide from 1992 to 1994. These officers were from all types and sizes of departments, including urban, suburban, and rural. Langston found that 37 percent of accidental police deaths were the result of suicide. Homicide was the second leading cause of accidental death at 26 percent, followed by motor vehicle accidents (26%) and other accidents (11%). Langston found that older officers committed suicide more often than younger ones did, with the most suicides occurring after the age of fifty-five. Guns were used in the majority of suicides. The average age of police suicide was 49.7 years. The significance of this study is that it was conducted on a wide geographical scale. It was, however, limited in its scope due to several factors. First, this study covered only three years of police policy claims. Most retrospective epidemiological mortality studies cover longer periods (twenty to twenty-five years for example) to get the full impact of exposure on the cohort involved. Two or three years may not indicate a true overall number, because some years may have higher or lower rates than others and not reflect a true picture of cohort death rates. Secondly, the study was conducted only on FOP members. Not all police officers in this country belong to the FOP.

Another problem concerns the accuracy of death records. Not all states record occupation on death certificates and the accuracy of those occupations that are recorded is at times questionable. Those persons listed as "police" on the death certificate may have only worked in policing for a short period of time, or the term police may have been interpreted differently across different medical examiner/coroner jurisdictions.

The reference group to which police suicide is compared presents an additional methodological problem. Many studies on suicide in general utilize the U.S. general population as a comparison group.

This may end in a biased result because the general population includes the unemployed, institutionalized, incarcerated, and mentally ill (Kramer, Pollack, Reddick & Locke, 1972). These population groups generally experience higher suicide rates. Thus, in essence, the police *should have relatively low suicide rates* when compared to the general population. The police are a physically and psychologically healthy working group, which can lead to a "healthy worker effect" bias (McMichael, 1976). Even if such a comparison were close to accurate, the fact that many studies show police officers to have a suicide rates equal to or higher than the general population suggests a cause for concern.

Measurement: Police Suicide Rates or Risk?

The majority of police suicide studies use a suicide rate per 100,000 to make comparisons and as a way to assess differences between groups. There is a difference between suicide *rates* and suicide *risk*. These measures reflect different aspects of mortality and should not be compared directly with one another (Greenberg, Daniels, Flanders, Eley & Boring, 1996). Rates are preferred if the assessment centers on how quickly (in time) new suicides arise. Risk is most useful if one wants to assess the probability that an individual will commit suicide over a specified period of time (e.g., a number of years). Generally, the word rate should be restricted to measures involving instantaneous changes and omit it from measures that can be viewed as proportions (Friedman, 1994).

Another way to assess risk is to determine the ratio for the rates of one group to another. The ratio of two rates is sometimes called the relative risk. The ratio of two rates is called the risk ratio. The latter term is usually used when mortality is compared to a standard or benchmark (such as the U.S. population). Two rates are also used in the equivalent ratio comparison of cases observed to case expected given the standard rates. When any of these ratios is calculated in a way that takes into account differences with respect to age or other characteristics, the ratio is said to be standardized – thus the term standardized rate ratio (SMR). Whether standardized or not, the ratio of two proportional mortality rates is the PMR (Friedman, 1994).

Will we better understand police suicide if we assess the risk of suicide in police work and not simply rates of suicide? How, then, do we assess the risk of suicide among police officers? This is a difficult question because the predictors of police suicide are not yet well-defined. To date, there have been no definitive studies that lay the foundation for police suicide risk predictors. We know that there are certain factors that occur more often than not in police suicides, but can they effectively predict such suicides? This is a crucial question for prevention. Psychological autopsies may help in this regard. Factors that are part of suicide risk assessment are believed to be better at predicting suicide than are other available measures. Some suicide risk factors are developed subjectively by asking knowledgeable professionals to select items their experience tells them are predictive. Other police measures are empirical, using statistical analyses to select among a set of available data elements that capture attributes of suicide (Gonzales, Henke & Flores, 2005).

Gonzales and colleagues (2005) provide five steps to be followed in developing a methodologically sound *risk* prediction:

- First, define the behavior or event to be predicted and develop procedures for classifying persons on the basis of their performance in regard to that behavior or event.
- Second, the attributes or characteristics on which the predictions may be based are selected and defined. Critics of prediction methods often argue that the procedures ignore differences among individuals. However, such differences, often assumed to be a source of error in other problems, are in fact the basis for any prediction effort. If the persons studied are alike with respect to the predictor candidates, no differential prediction can be made. If they are alike with respect to the criterion categories, there is no prediction problem.
- The third step is to determine relationships between predictor variables and criteria in a sample representative of the population for which inferences are to be drawn.
- Fourth, the relations found in the original sample must be verified by testing the prediction procedures in a new sample, or samples, of the population. Although this verification (cross-validation) often is omitted, it is a critical step.
- Fifth, the prediction method may be applied in situations for which it was developed, provided that the stability of predictions has been supported in the cross-validation step and appropriate samples have been used. (Gonzales, Henke & Flores, 2005).

Because no precise prediction of police suicide (or any suicide for that matter) can be made with certainty, a statement of probability (risk) may be more appropriate than a rate. Predictions are properly applied to groups of persons who are similar in terms of some set of characteristics, rather than to individuals. In any prediction problem, individuals are assigned to classes, and then statements are made about the expected performance of members of the classes. For specific classifications of persons, the expected outcomes ought to be those that provide the most probable values for those classes. This, of course, leads to another difficulty in prediction. Suicide is an individual decision, and making statements about the police as a group does not afford a reliable model for prevention. As Gonzales and associates (2005) stated, the validity of prediction refers to the relation between an earlier assessment and a specific criterion measure, and it depends on the particular criterion used. Evidence of validity with respect to a specific criterion of interest in the police obviously is necessary before any practical application of the method.

CONCLUSION

Given the present state of research on the police, it is likely that inaccuracies will continue to exist. Underreporting, misclassification, the lack of nationwide updated comprehensive data, and the difficulty associated with collecting data leaves us with this choice. Exposure and job socialization in policing have profound impacts on officers. Exactly how to measure the impact that police work has on individuals over time is a difficult question. It will likely take long-term prospective studies to make sense out of such exposure.

REFERENCES

Aamodt, M. G., & Stalnaker, N. A. (2001). Police officer suicide: Frequency and officer profiles. In D. C. Sheehan and J. I. Warren (Eds.), *Suicide and Law Enforcement* (pp. 383–398). Washington, DC: US Government Printing Office.

Alpert, G. P., & Dunham, R. G. (1988). *Policing urban America.* Prospect Heights, IL: Waveland.

Berg, A. M., Hem, E., Lau, B., Loeb, M., & Ekeberg, O. (2003). Suicidal ideation and attempts in Norwegian police. *Suicide and Life-Threatening Behavior, 33*, 302–312.
Burnett, C. A., Boxer, P. A., & Swanson, N. G. (1992). *Suicide and occupation: Is there a relationship?*, Paper presented at the American Psychological Association–National Institute for Occupational Health Conference, Washington, DC, November 19–22.
Cantor, C. H., Tyman, R., & Slater, P. J. (1995). A historical survey of police in Queensland, Australia, 1843–1992. *Suicide and Life-Threatening Behavior, 25*, 499–507.
Charbonneau, F. (2000). Suicide among the police in Quebec. *Population, 55*, 367–378.
Darragh, P. M. (1991). Epidemiology of suicide in Northern Ireland. *Irish Journal of Medical Science, 160*, 354–357.
Dash, J., & Reiser, M. (1978). Suicide among police in urban law enforcement agencies. *Journal of Police Science and Administration, 6*, 18–21.
Forastiere, F., Perucci, C. A., DiPietro, A., Miceli, M., Rapiti, E., Bargagli, A., & Borgia, P. (1994). Mortality among urban policemen in Rome. *American Journal of Industrial Medicine, 26*, 785–798.
Friedman, G. D. (1994). *Primer for Epidemiology*. New York: McGraw-Hill.
Gershon, R. R., Lin, S., & Li, X. (2002). Work stress in aging police officers. *Journal of Occupational and Environmental Medicine, 44*, 160–167.
Gonzales, A. R., Henke, T. A., & Flores, J. R. (2005). *The Mathematics of Risk Classification: Changing Data Into Valid Instruments for Juvenile Courts*. Office of Justice Programs. (NCJ 209158, pp. 1–6). Washington, DC: U.S. Department of Justice.
Greenberg, R. S., Daniels, S. R., Flanders, D. W., Eley, J. W., & Boring, J. R. (1996). *Medical Epidemiology*. Stanford, CT: Appleton & Lange.
Hartwig, D., & Violanti, J. M. (1999). Suicide by police officials in North Rhine-Westphalia. An evaluation of 58 suicide between 1992–1998. *Archives of Kriminologie, 204*, 129–142.
Heiman, M. F. (1977). Suicide among police. *American Journal of Psychiatry, 134*, 1288.
Helmkamp, J. C. (1996). Occupation and suicide among males in the US Armed Forces. *Annals of Epidemiology, 6*, 83–88.
Hem, E., Berg, A. M., & Ekeberg, O. (2001). Suicide in police – A critical review. *Suicide and Life-Threatening Behavior, 31*, 224–233.
Jenkins, E. L. (2005). Suicide. In B. S. Levy, G. R. Wagner, K. M. Rest, and J. L. Weeks (Eds.), *Preventing occupational disease and injury* (2nd ed.). (pp. 473–475). Washington, DC: American Public Health Association.
Johnson, D. L. (1995). *Workplace violence: Practical strategies involving EAPs and mental health professionals*. Symposium conducted at the Work, Stress and Health Conference, September 1995, Washington, DC.
Josephson, R. L., & Reiser, M. (1990). Officer suicide in the Los Angeles police department: A twelve year follow-up. *Journal of Police Science and Administration, 17*, 227–229.
Kappeler, V. E., Blumberg, M., & Potter, G. W. (1993). *The mythology of crime and criminal justice* (pp. 134–136). Prospect Heights, IL: Waveland.

Kramer, M., Pollack, E., Reddick, R., & Locke, B. (1972). *Mental disorders/suicide.* Cambridge, MA: Harvard University Press.
Langston, E. (1995). *Police Suicide.* Presentation at American Criminal Justice Society Annual Conference. March 1995, Boston, Massachusetts.
Lester, D. (1992). Suicide in police officers: A survey of nations. *Police Studies, 15,* 146–148.
Loo, R. (2003). A meta-analysis of police suicide rates: Findings and issues. *Suicide and Life-Threatening Behavior, 33,* 313–325.
Marzuk, P. M., Nock, M. K., Leon, A. C., Portera, L., & Tardiff, K. (2002). Suicide among New York City police officers, 1977–1996. *American Journal of Psychiatry, 159,* 2069–2071.
McMichael, A. J. (1976). Standardized mortality ratios and the healthy worker effect: Scratching beneath the surface. *Journal of Occupational Medicine, 18,* 165–168.
Milham, S. (1979). *Occupational mortality in Washington state.* U.S. Department of Health, Education, and Welfare, 1-3. Washington, DC: US Government Printing Office.
National Institute for Occupational Safety and Health [NIOSH]. (1993). *Fatal injuries to workers in the United States, 1980–1989: A decade of surveillance* (DHHS NIOSH No. 93-108). Cincinnati, OH: NIOSH.
Reaves, B. A. (2003). Census of state and local law enforcement agencies, 2000. *Bureau of Justice Statistics Bulletin, 1,* 15.
Rothman, S., & Strijdom, S. (2002). Suicide ideation in the South African Police Services in the Northwest province. *South African Journal of Industrial Psychology, 28,* 44–48.
Stack, S., & Kelley, T. (1994). Police suicide: An analysis. *American Journal of Police, XIII,* 73–90.
Vena, J. E., Violanti, J. M., Marshall, J. R., & Feidler, F. (1986). Mortality of a municipal worker cohort III: Police officers. *Journal of Industrial Medicine, 10,* 383–397.
Violanti, J. M. (2004). Predictors of police suicide ideation. *Suicide and Life-Threatening Behavior, 4,* 277–283.
Violanti, J. M. (in press). Suicide or undetermined? A national assessment of police suicide death classification. *International Journal of Emergency Mental Health.*
Violanti, J. M., Fekedulegn, D., Charles, L. E., Andrew, M. E., Hartley, T. A., Mnatsakanova, A., & Burchfiel, C. M. (2008). *Depression and Suicidal Ideation Among Police Officers.* Presentation at the Work, Stress, and Health Conference, March, 2008, Washington, DC.
Violanti, J. M., Vena, J. E., & Marshall, J. R. (1996). Suicides, homicides, and accidental deaths: A comparative risk assessment of police officers and municipal workers. *American Journal of Industrial Medicine, 30,* 99–104.
Violanti, J. M., Vena, J. E., & Petralia, S. (1998). Mortality of a police cohort: 1950–1990. *American Journal of Industrial Medicine, 33,* 366–373.

Chapter 2

RECENT NATIONAL STUDIES ON POLICE SUICIDE

JOHN M. VIOLANTI and ANDREW F. O'HARA

INTRODUCTION

The objective of this chapter is to describe police suicide rates on a national level in the United States. Our first study describes a national surveillance of police suicide rates utilizing data from the CDC and compares those rates with similar occupations (firefighters and military) (Violanti, 2010). In their work, firefighters are exposed to many traumatic events that are similar to what police officers experience (Corneil et al., 1999). Examples are dead bodies, severely injured persons, and human misery. Military personnel are similar to police in that they must be under constant vigilance for the "enemy" and in danger of death from unsuspected sources. They are also under similar types of rank structure and have ready access to firearms (Mahon, Tobin, Cusack, Kelleher & Malone, 2005; Violanti & Paton, 1998). A second objective was to examine police suicide rates in women and minority officers. Little is known about gender and ethnic differences in police suicide. The second study involves a national web surveillance of all media-reported police suicide for the year 2008 (O'Hara & Violanti, 2009).

STUDY ONE: CDC NATIONAL DATA ON POLICE, FIREFIGHTER, AND MILITARY SUICIDE

We utilized NOMS as a data source. NIOSH maintains the NOMS system database of death certificate data with standard coded occupation and industry information. Twenty-eight states (Alaska, Colorado, Georgia, Hawaii, Idaho, Indiana, Kansas, Kentucky, Maine, Missouri, Nebraska, Nevada, New Hampshire, New Jersey, New Mexico, New York, North Carolina, Ohio, Oklahoma, Pennsylvania, Rhode Island, South Carolina, Tennessee, Utah, Vermont, Washington, West Virginia, and Wisconsin) have participated in the project for two or more years from 1984 to 1998 (Burnett, Maurer, Rosenberg & Dosemeci, 1997). NOMS includes more than 8.5 million death certificates collected during the period from 1984 to 1998. Although the NOMS database lacks information on length of employment, specificity of job description, or estimates of workplace exposures, its advantages include its size and its broad geographic coverage and the recent date of death of cases. Depending on date of death, the usual occupation of the decedent is coded according to the 1980 and 1990 Bureau of the Census classification system (U.S. Bureau of Census, 1980, 1990). Cause of death is coded according to the ninth revision of the International Classification of Diseases (ICD-9) (World Health Organization, 1977).

We limited our examination to occupational categories "police and detectives" and "police supervisors" (occupation codes 414, 418–424), "firefighters" (occupation codes 413, 416, 417), and "military personnel" (occupation code 905). ICD-9 codes 950 to 959 "suicide and self-inflicted injury" were used for suicide classification across the three occupational groups and twenty-eight states. The measure of association used most often in NOMS is the PMR (Kupper, McMichael, Symons & Most, 1978). The PMR indicates whether the age-standardized proportion of deaths from a specific cause of death for a particular occupation appears to be higher or lower than the expected proportion for that particular occupation. PMRs are generally used with NOMS data because no comparable population information exists to calculate rates. Age stratification is done in five-year age groups. To test for statistical significance of the PMR, two-sided 95 percent CIs were calculated based on the Poisson distribution for observed deaths and using the normal approximation to the Poisson for large numbers.

A PMR greater than 100 indicates that more deaths than expected were associated with the condition in an occupation.

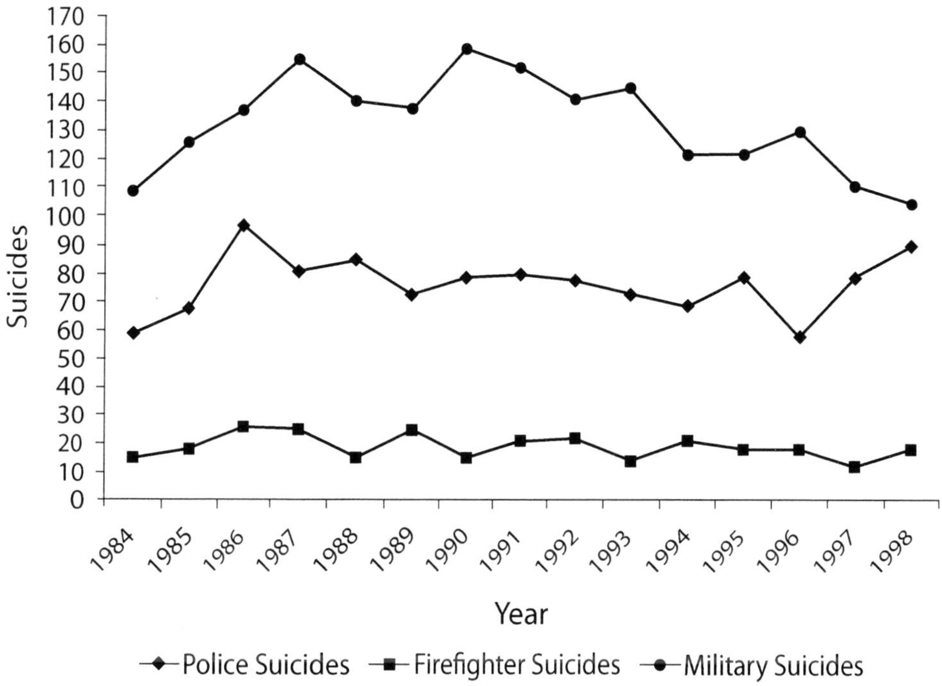

Figure 2–1. Police, Firefighter, and Military Suicides by Year. CDC/NOMS Data 1994–1998.

Figure 2–1 represents the total number of suicides by year for police, firefighters, and military personnel from 1984 to 1998. Military personnel had the highest mean number of suicides per year followed by police and firefighters in that order (military = 116; police = 77; firefighters = 17). The yearly data indicate a fairly constant pattern of suicides across these three occupations, with the exception of the police, who show an upward trend in the number of suicides in 1998 (n = 90).

A five-year interval breakdown by gender and ethnicity for suicide across police, military, and firefighters is presented in Table 2–1. In terms of total number of suicides across the three occupations, the police had approximately four times the number of suicides than did firefighters, but not more than military personnel. Suicide in all three occupations decreased slightly in percentage from 1984 to 1998; how-

Table 2–1.
Suicide by Five-Year Categories Across Gender, Ethnicity, and Occupation, 1984–1998.

	Caucasian				African American					
	Men		Women		Men		Women		Totals*	
	N	%	N	%	N	%	N	%	N	%
POLICE & DETECTIVES										
1984–1988	354	35.47	12	20.33	20	25.00	4	36.36	390	33.97
1989–1993	325	32.55	21	35.59	32	40.00	5	45.45	383	33.36
1994–1998	319	31.96	26	44.06	28	35.00	2	18.18	375	32.66
Totals	998	99.98	59	99.98	80	100.00	11	99.99	1148	99.99
FIREFIGHTERS, FIRE PREVENTION OCCUPATIONS										
1984–1988	90	34.62	3	60.00	6	33.34	–	–	99	34.98
1989–1993	88	33.85	2	40.00	7	38.90	–	–	97	30.73
1994–1998	82	31.53	–	–	3	16.68	–	–	87	30.74
Totals	260	100.00	5	100.00	18	88.92	–	–	283	96.45
MILITARY PERSONNEL										
1984–1988	585	33.73	15	28.85	66	32.83	2	33.33	668	33.51
1989–1993	637	36.74	25	48.07	72	35.83	1	16.67	735	36.88
1994–1998	512	29.53	12	23.07	63	31.35	3	50.00	590	29.60
Totals	1734	100.00	52	99.99	201	100.00	6	100.00	1993	99.99

* Some totals not 100% due to rounding and missing data

ever, the police had the least amount of decrease (police = 1.30%; fire = 4.24%; military = 3.91%), indicating a more consistent level of suicides.

White male police had approximately 3.8 times the number of suicides as did male firefighters. Among white males, there does not appear to be a significant change in the percentage of suicides per five-year period. Black male police had approximately 4.5 times the number of suicides as firefighters and the highest number of suicides between 1989 and 1993 (n = 32), showing a slight decrease in the subsequent five-year period from 1994 to 1998 (n = 28).

White female police had approximately twelve times the number of suicides as female firefighters. White female police officers showed an increasing pattern of suicides from 1984 to 1998 (20.3% during 1984 to 1988 to 44.06% during 1994 to 1998), whereas white female firefighter and military personnel showed an inconsistent pattern. The number for black female personnel was small and showed inconsistent patterns in the number of suicides across the fifteen-year period.

Table 2–2 compares age category, gender, and ethnicity for suicides across the three occupations. In general, the majority of suicides occurred among the younger age groups (ages 21–30: police = 20.8%; military = 29%; firefighters = 10.6%). Approximately 18.34 percent of suicides for male police and 33.9 percent for female police occurred in the twenty-one to thirty age group. This trend was apparent across gender and ethnicity and among military personnel but not firefighters.

PMRs for suicide are presented in Table 2–3, expressed in gender and ethnicity categories across police, firefighters, and military personnel. In total, white and black police men and women exhibited significant PMRs for suicide. White men had a PMR of 120 (n = 998; p <0.01; 95% CI = 113–128); white women had a PMR of 206 (n = 59; p <0.01; 95% CI = 157–265); black men had a PMR of 203 (n = 76; p <0.01; 95% CI = 161–252); and black women had a PMR of 415 (n = 11; p <0.01; 95% CI = 207–742). Similar results were found among military personnel, but not firefighters. Of the three occupations, police had the highest PMRs for suicide.

Several conclusions are suggested by these results. On average, police suicide rates were somewhat lower in the NOMS data (mean = 77 per year) than have been reported recently by the national media and by various police suicide benevolent organizations. This does not

Table 2–2.
Suicide Across Age, Gender, Ethnicity, and Occupation, 1984–1998.

	Caucasian				African American					
Age	Men		Women		Men		Women		Totals	
	N	%	N	%	N	%	N	%	N	%
POLICE & DETECTIVES										
21–30	183	18.34	20	33.90	30	37.50	6	54.55	239	20.82
31–39	168	16.83	18	30.51	25	31.25	4	36.36	215	18.73
40–49	196	19.64	12	20.34	15	18.75	–	–	223	19.43
50–59	148	14.83	6	10.17	5	6.25	–	–	159	13.85
60–69	138	13.83	2	3.39	2	2.50	1	9.09	143	12.46
70+	165	16.53	1	1.69	3	3.75	–	–	169	14.72
FIREFIGHTERS, FIRE PREVENTION OCCUPATIONS										
21–30	21	8.08	2	40.00	7	38.89	–	–	30	10.60
31–39	45	17.31	1	20.00	7	38.89	–	–	53	18.73
40–49	50	19.23	2	40.00	3	16.67	–	–	55	19.43
50–59	50	19.23	–	–	–	–	–	–	50	17.67
60–69	40	15.38	–	–	1	5.56	–	–	41	14.49
70+	54	20.77	–	–	–	–	–	–	54	19.08
MILITARY PERSONNEL										
21–30	457	26.36	28	53.85	91	45.27	3	50.00	579	29.05
31–39	237	13.67	10	19.23	57	28.36	2	33.33	306	15.35
40–49	251	14.48	7	13.46	31	15.42	1	16.67	290	14.55
50–59	228	13.15	2	3.85	6	2.99	–	–	236	11.84
60–69	301	17.36	4	7.69	9	4.48	–	–	314	15.76
70+	260	14.99	1	1.92	7	3.48	–	–	268	13.45

Table 2–3.

Proportionate Mortality Ratios – Suicide (Police, Firefighters, and Military) by Age, Gender, and Ethnicity, 1984–1998.

Age	Caucasian						African American					
	Men			Women			Men			Women		
	N	PMR	95% CI	N	PMR	95% CI	N	PMR	95% CI	N	PMR	95% CI
POLICE & DETECTIVES												
21–64	765	115**	107–124	57	215**	163–279	76	206**	162–258	11	430**	215–769
65–120	233	138**	121–157	2	92	11–331	4	157	43–403	–	–	–
Total	998	120**	113–128	59	206**	157–265	80	203**	161–252	11	415**	207–742
FIREFIGHTERS, FIRE PREVENTION OCCUPATIONS												
21–64	182	101	87–116	5	259	84–604	18	244**	145–386	–	–	–
65–120	78	109	86–136	0	0	0–2944	0	0	0–683	–	–	–
Total	260	103	91–116	5	243	79–567	18	228**	135–360	–	–	–
MILITARY PERSONNEL												
21–64	1323	106**	101–111	49	179**	132–236	189	175**	151–202	6	191	70–415
65–120	411	122**	111–135	3	171	35–500	12	165	85–288	–	–	–
Total	1734	110**	105–114	52	178**	133–234	201	175**	151–201	6	189	69–411

** p <0.01

Military deaths n = 74, 860

Police deaths n = 40, 188

Firefighter deaths n = 14, 184

detract from the seriousness of police suicide, however. Although we cannot accurately predict rates beyond the present data, there appears to be an upward trend in the number of police suicides. In comparing the total number of suicides across the three occupations, the police had approximately four times the number of suicides than did firefighters, but not more than military personnel. Suicide in all three occupations decreased slightly in percentage from 1984 to1998; however, the police had the least amount of decrease (police = 1.3%; fire = 4.24%; military = 3.91%), indicating a more consistent level of suicides to 1998.

Lacking in the literature on police suicide are national data on ethnicities and gender. We found that white male police had approximately 3.8 times the number of suicides than did male firefighters. Black male police officers had the highest number of suicides in the period 1989 to 1993 (n = 32), showing a slight decreasing number in the subsequent five-year period 1994 to 1998 (n = 28). Despite this slight decrease, black police men had approximately 4.5 times the number of suicides than did male firefighters. Research suggests that minority police officers have different attitudes toward police work and report inadequate support as an emergent stressor (Dowler, 2005; Haar & Morash, 1999). Dowler (2005) reported that black officers are more likely to feel criticized and to believe that they are perceived as militant. In essence, there exists sense of isolation among minority officers that can exacerbate burnout and depression (Polk, 1995). These are precipitants for suicide.

White female police had approximately twelve times the number of suicides as did female firefighters and showed an increasing trend of suicide from 1984 to 1998 (20.3% during 1984–1988 to 44.06% during 1994–1998). Although the numbers of suicide were small, they lend some credence to the possible negative psychological consequences of policing on women (Dormann & Zapf, 2002). An alternative explanation may be an increasing proportion of women in police work from 1984 to 1998. However, such an increase does not appear to be sufficiently large enough to negate the increase in suicides. According to the National Center for Women and Policing (2001), women gained only approximately one half of a percentage point per year in their representation within police agencies from 1972 to 1999, and there is mounting evidence that this trend has now stalled or even reversed. In 2001, women accounted for only 12.7 percent of all sworn law enforcement positions in police agencies, a figure that is less than four percentage points higher than in 1990, when women composed 9 percent of sworn officers. White female firefighter and military personnel showed an inconsistent suicide pattern. Black women were small in number and showed inconsistent patterns of suicide across the fifteen-year period.

Age is an important risk factor associated with suicide. In the United States, persons in the younger age groups composed 14.2 percent of the population and accounted for 16.6 percent of suicides (National Vital Statistics Reports, 2005). These data indicated a higher percentage of suicides among younger police officers. This is a disturbing trend. Within ethnic and gender groups, the majority of suicides also occurred among the younger ages, with the exception of firefighters. Among white and black police men and women, there appeared to be an inverse pattern associated with age, with the highest proportion of suicides occurring in younger age groups. Approximately 18.34 percent of suicides for male police and 33.9 percent for female police occurred in the 21 to 30 age group. Similar results were seen among military personnel.

PMRs for suicide were presented in Table 2–3 and were expressed in gender and ethnicity categories across police, firefighters, and military personnel. A PMR greater than 100 indicates that more deaths are associated with suicide in an occupation than was expected. In total, both white and black police men and women exhibited significant PMRs for suicide. White men had a PMR of 120 ($n = 998$; $p < 0.01$; 95% CI = 113–128) and women had a PMR of 206 ($n = 59$; $p < 0.01$; 95% CI = 157–265), whereas black men had a PMR of 203 ($n = 80$; $p < 0.01$; 95% CI = 161–252) and women had a PMR of 415 ($n = 11$; $p < 0.01$; 95% CI = 207–742). Stated differently, white male police had a significant (20%) increased risk of suicide, white women a significant (200%) increased risk, black police men a significant (200%) increased risk, and black women a significant (400%) increased risk for suicide. Similar increased PMRs were found among military personnel, but not firefighters. Of the three occupations, police had the highest PMRs for suicide.

There are limitations to the present study. NOMS data are presently available up to 1998, and national information on police suicides is not available from that year until the present. As seen in Figure 2–1, there appears to be an increasing number of police suicides in the latest time period available in NOMS. This suggests a future trend of increasing suicides among police. We cannot predict this trend beyond the data available, however. Updating of the NOMS database will help to determine whether police suicide rates have substantially increased since the last available data. Updated national data will also add information for military suicide, which is even higher than police suicide. The impact of recent exposure to the wars in Iraq and Afghanistan has already led to speculation that suicide among the military is reaching epidemic proportions (Hoge et al., 2004). Additionally, police officers in the military reserve returning from war zones may also be at increased suicide risk.

STUDY TWO: A NATIONAL WEB SURVEILLANCE STUDY OF MEDIA REPORTS ON POLICE SUICIDE

The expansive societal use of the internet proved to be of great advantage in our research. It is clear that in this age of vast, rapidly interlinking communications, a police suicide in even the smallest and most remote community is not only reported in that local area but also, given both public and media interest in the subject, reported by multiple media in a chain reaction that lasts several days to several weeks. Adding to the repetitious spread of these reports on the internet are the dozens of police websites, forums and blogs, which are quick to re-report the event. This has greatly reduced the likelihood that a police suicide will go unnoticed.

News media internet reports provide a reliable means of establishing when, where, and why police suicides were occurring during a given year. Rainey and Runyan (1992) found that relying solely on news reports for information on fire- and drowning-related deaths would result in a 96 percent and 72 percent, respectively, capture rate of reports. Further, the consistent application of the same surveillance terms throughout the year in our surveillance did much to ensure consistency of data gathering throughout 2008. Approximately 119,000 suicide-specific news articles were reviewed during the year for information relating to police suicides in the United States (O'Hara & Violanti, 2009). In this chapter, we have added data for 2009 not yet published.

Descriptive information for this surveillance is displayed in Table 2–4. The data yielded ages for fifty-nine officers who had committed suicide during 2008. Ages for the remaining forty-three officers were accepted as due to either the shortage of information given by the department or incomplete reporting by the media. In an effort to find a workable age where one was missing, we relied on a median derived from two tables provided by the Illinois State Police (Raub, 1987) and the State of Nevada Public Employees Retirement System. By taking an average service retirement of age fifty-five and a hypothetical hiring age of twenty-one, a median age would be age thirty-eight years of age. In looking at the earlier spread of ages and seeing the known average age of the fifty-nine officers to be 40.1 years of age, we felt that thirty-eight was in a comfortable range for use with those officers lacking an identified age.

Using the same criteria for missing years of police service, we initially identified and attempted to use seventeen years as a median work time (seventeen simply being between a hire date of twenty-one and a service retirement of fifty-five. The resultant adjusted time on the job was seventeen years.) Time on the job was given in articles for forty officers, with an average time on the job of thirteen years. Even though the distribution of years on the job was relatively uniform, we chose nonetheless to use the average time on the job (thirteen years) of those provided in the raw data as being more realistic. In cases in which the officer clearly had less than thirteen years on the job, we used the smaller number based on a presumed hire age of twenty-one (example, a twenty-three–year-old officer was presumed, for this study, to have two years on the job). Suicides by officers separated from their employment by less than one year and exhibiting behaviors likely predictive of suicide attributable to their employment were included within the study.

The data across 2008 and 2009 remained fairly consistent. Those who committed suicide in 2009 were on average older and had more years of service. In 2009, suicide among the thirty-five to thirty-nine years of age category appeared to decrease, whereas increasing slightly in the forty to forty-four year category. Suicide by firearm remained the primary method.

This study attempted to provide a recent descriptive view of police suicide rates in the United States. Results indicated that 102 actual police suicides were accounted for in 2008 and 104 in 2009 via web

Table 2-4.

Descriptive Data – Police Suicide Web Surveillance 2008 and 2009.

Year	2008 (n = 102)		2009 (n = 104)	
	N	(%)	N	(%)
Gender				
Male	93	(91.2%)	97	(3.3%)
Female	7	(9.8%)	6	(5.8%)
Age	(n = 59, Mean = 38.7 years)		(n = 44, Mean = 42.7 years)	
20–24	2	(3%)	1	(1%)
25–29	7	(12%)	3	(6.8%)
30–34	3	(5%)	4	(9.1%)
35–39	17	(29%)	6	(13.6%)
40–44	11	(19%)	12	(27.3%)
45–49	10	(17%)	3	(6.8%)
50–54	4	(7%)	7	(15.9%)
55+	5	(8%)	5	(11.3%)
Years Police Service	(n = 40, Mean = 12.2 years)		(n = 41, Mean = 17 years)	
0–4	7	(17%)	4	(9.7%)
5–9	4	(10%)	3	(7.3%)
10–14	9	(22%)	8	(2.4%)
15–19	7	(17%)	4	(9.8%)
20–24	7	(17%)	11	(26.8%)
25+	6	(15%)	10	(24.4%)
Rank				
Below Sergeant	89	(88.7%)	89	(89.3%)
Above Sergeant	11	(11.3%)	14	(13.5%)
Method				
Gunshot	136	(96.1%)	77	(91.4%)
Hanging	3	(1.9%)	1	(1.2%)
Auto	1	(0.97%)	–	–
Overdose	1	(0.97%)	4	(4.8%)
Carbon Monoxide	–	–	1	(1.2%)
Knife	–	–	1	(1.2%)

surveillance hits. If we consider two assumptions, the rate may be higher than we determined. The first assumption is that approximately 17 percent of police suicides are either misclassified as accidents or undetermined deaths (Violanti, 2007). The second assumption was that we possibly missed approximately 20 percent of suicides due to our own review process or researcher error or by news articles that conceivably might not have been fed into the internet. The latter assumption is robust, given the intensity of our review process and our observation during the year that police suicides are of high media interest, are reported by multiple news media from surrounding communities (press and television), and thus will almost inevitably appear in articles by other media repeated times – often for weeks. If we take these assumptions into consideration, the final count would be approximately 141 police suicides. This figure is surprisingly consistent with CDC/NOMS data and other current research (Violanti, 2007). We cannot verify this total without further investigation of accidental or undetermined police mortality data. Future research and the use of psychological autopsy methodology may help to clarify this data.

In terms of other results, it appears that officers in the age category thirty to thirty-five years are at a higher risk for suicide, with 29 percent of all suicides found in this age group. Additionally, those officers with ten to fourteen years of service are at an increase risk for suicide. Suicide among officers of lower rank and the use of firearms were prevalent.

These results are significant in terms of prevention. Twelve percent of officers showed clear warning signs of potential suicide that went unnoticed, whereas 64 percent of officers appeared to have slipped completely "under the radar," showing no noticeable signs or symptoms of distress before taking their lives. The latter is significant and highlights the ability of an officer to maintain a facade, a "front," before his peers. Law enforcement has its own code of conduct and subculture, and officers feel a need to disguise signs of psychological distress for fear of being perceived as "soft" or weak (Arrigo & Shipley, 2004). Additionally, the high percentage of reportedly missed suicides would imply that officers are far more adept at disguising their intentions than previously expected (Slovenko, 2002).

Discussions have suggested that police work, over many years, has its comparisons to the shorter tours of duty (albeit more frequent today) by the military in a war zone. Without debating the merits of that premise, however, we compared suicides in the United States Army, with a population of 675,000 soldiers, with that of police officers, population 861,000. The Army reported 128 suicides in 2008 (with 15 still pending) (U.S. Army, 2009) compared to the 141 we found for law enforcement in that same year. We found the two remarkably consistent.

There are limitations to this research. Although web-based surveillance is a fairly reliable source, the use of actual mortality statistics based on death certificates and autopsy reports are a best source. Unfortunately, nationwide collection of such data is a long and difficult task. The cooperation of police departments across the country is essential if this is to be accomplished in future research. Despite limitations, our year-long surveillance of more than 119,000 suicide-related news reports, followed by properly designed adjustments and accommodation for variables, yielded data consistent not only with past CDC/NOMS data, but also with independent reporting by a wide variety of police publications that take intense interest in the topic of police suicides.

REFERENCES

Arrigo, B. A., & Shipley, S. L., (2004). *Introduction to forensic psychology: Issues and controversies in crime and justice* (2nd ed.). Burlington, MA: Academic Press.

Burnett, C., Maurer, J., Rosenberg, H. M., & Dosemeci, M. (1997). *Mortality by occupation, industry, and cause of death: 24 reporting states (1984–1988).* (NIOSH 97–114). Cincinnati, OH: NIOSH, U. S. Department of Health and Human Services, Cincinnati, Ohio, DHHS (NIOSH) Publication No. 97–114.

Corneil, D. W., Beaton, R., Murphy, S., Johnson, C., & Pike, K. (1999). Exposure to traumatic incidents and prevalence of post-traumatic stress disorder symptomatology in urban firefighter in two countries. *Journal of Occupational Health Psychology, 4,* 131–141.

Dormann, C., & Zapf, D. (2002). Social stressors at work, irritation and depressive symptoms: Accounting for unmeasured third variables in a multi-wave study. *Journal of Occupational and Organization Psychology, 75,* 33–58.

Dowler, K. (2005). Job satisfaction, burnout, and perception of unfair treatment: The relationship between race and police work. *Police Quarterly, 8,* 476–489.

Hoge, C. W., Castro, C. A., Messer, S. C., McGurk, D., Cotting, D. I., & Koffman, R. L. (2004). Combat duty in Iraq and Afghanistan, metal health problems and barriers to care. *New England Journal of Medicine, 351,* 13–22.

Kupper L. L., McMichael A. J., Symons M. J., & Most, B. M. (1978). On the utility of proportional mortality analysis. *Journal of Chronic Disease, 31,* 15–22.

Mahon, M. J., Tobin, J. P., Cusack, D. A., Kelleher, C., & Malone, K. M. (2005). Suicide among regular-duty military personnel: A retrospective case-control study of occupation-specific factors for workplace suicide. *The American Journal of Psychiatry, 162,* 1688–1696.

National Center for Women and Policing. (2001). *The status of women in policing.* Washington, DC: Author.

O'Hara, A., & Violanti, J. M. (2009). Police suicide: A web surveillance of national data. *International Journal of Emergency Mental Health, 11,* 17–24.

Polk, O. E. (1995). The effects of ethnicity on career paths of advanced/specialized law enforcement officers. *American Journal of Police, 18*, 1–21.
Rainey, D. Y., & Runyan, C. W. (1992). A source for injury surveillance. *American Journal of Public Health, 82*, 745–746.
Raub, R. A. (1987). *Police officer retirement: The beginning of a long life*. Washington, DC: National Institute of Justice Publication.
Slovenko, R. (2002). *Psychiatry in law/Law in psychiatry*. Vol. 2 (p. 784). New York: Taylor & Francis.
U. S. Army. (2009). *U.S. Army Releases 2008 Suicide Data, Highlights Efforts to Prevent Suicide,* Media Relations Division. Washington, DC: OCPA.
U. S. Bureau of the Census. (1992). *1980 Census of Population: Alphabetical Index of Industries and Occupations*. Washington, DC: U.S. Government Printing Office, 1980; U. S. Bureau of the Census. *1990 Census of Population and Housing: Alphabetical Index of Industries and Occupations*. Washington, DC: U.S. Government Printing Office.
Violanti, J. M., & Paton, D. (1998). *Police trauma: Psychological aftermath of civilian combat*. Springfield, IL: Charles C Thomas.
Violanti, J. M. (2007). *Police suicide, epidemic in blue* (pp. 46–50). Springfield, IL: Charles C Thomas.
Violanti, J. M. (2010). Police suicide: A national comparison with firefighter and military personnel. DOI 10.1108/13639511011044885. *Policing: An International Journal of Police Strategies & Management, 33*, 270–286.
World Health Organization. (1977). *International Classification of Diseases. Manual of the International Statistical Classification of Diseases, Injuries, and Causes of Death. Based on the Recommendations of the Ninth Revision Conference, 1975*. Geneva: World Health Organization.

Chapter 3

PATHWAYS TO POLICE SUICIDE: TRAUMA STRESS ACROSS THE CAREER

JOHN M. VIOLANTI

INTRODUCTION

There is a need to look at predictors of police suicide. One strategy would be to examine lifelong or career-long factors that increase the risk of suicide among police officers. This chapter will explore this issue in the context of trauma exposure and life-course analysis.

Trauma and Suicide

PTSD is a unique set of symptoms brought about by exposure to a traumatic event that compromises the physical integrity or life of an individual and produces intense fear (American Psychiatric Association, 1994). The response includes symptomatology lasting at least one month and includes reliving the traumatic experience, avoidance of stimuli associated with the trauma or psychic numbing, and hyperarousal and physiological reactivity to events resembling the trauma.

PTSD is often associated with increased suicidal ideation. Marshall, Olfson, Hellman, Blanco, and Struening (2001) found that persons diagnosed with PTSD had a threefold risk of suicide ideation compared to those without PTSD. The high risk of ideation remained even when depression was controlled. Freeman, Roca, and Moore (2000) found that combat veterans with PTSD had significantly more suicide attempts and self-destructive behaviors.

Studies of veterans with PTSD have reported an increased risk of suicidal behavior; 82.6 percent of veterans in outpatient treatment reported symptoms of suicidal ideation (Davidson, Hughes, Blazer & George, 1991; Hendin & Haas, 1991). Moreover, a high preponderance of anxiety disorders, particularly PTSD, has been found in veterans with completed suicide relative to the general population of completed suicides (Lehmann, McCormick & McCracken, 1995). The incidence of PTSD was higher among Vietnam veterans who had killed themselves than among those who were killed in motor vehicle accidents (Farberow, Kang & Bullman, 1990). These results found the incidence of suicide to be higher in victims who met diagnostic criteria for PTSD than among victims who did not. In a study of refugees, suicidal behavior was significantly greater among victims with a diagnosis of PTSD than among non-PTSD victims (Ferrada-Noli, Asberg, Ormstad, Lundin & Sundbom, 1998).

Many persons diagnosed with PTSD have comorbid difficulties (Green, Lindy & Grace, 1989). For example, in a study of Vietnam veterans with PTSD, Roszell, McFall, and Malas (1991) found that nearly 50 percent indicated a current sense or belief of foreshortened future, and more than 64 percent had a current coexisting diagnosis of major depression (93% were currently diagnosed with some form of mood disorder).

Police Suicide and PTSD

Many work-related exposures of police officers are often characterized as traumatic compared to most other occupations (Paton, Violanti & Smith, 2003). Exposures perceived as "disturbing" or "traumatic" are generally ranked by police officers as the most stressful. Law enforcement officers are confronted daily with the reality of trauma. Faced with responding to fatal accidents, crime, child abuse, homicide, suicide, and rape, police officers are exposed to all the potential factors that can precipitate a traumatic response (Carlier, Fouwels, Lamberts & Gersons, 1996). There is also an increased risk of trauma due to frequent exposure to death and the threat of death (Sugimoto & Oltjenbruns, 2001).

Posttraumatic symtomatology can produce many negative consequences, including increased alcohol use and suicide among police officers. Being the target of, exposed to, as well as witness to events that can precipitate a sense of horror, helplessness, and hopelessness, it is not surprising that police officers have been empirically found to suffer the mental injuries associated with traumatic stress (Dunning, 1996). The ways that trauma can affect the police are wide ranging. To begin with, there are the effects on the traumatized officers themselves. Immediately after a traumatic experience, they tend to exhibit a cluster of characteristic reactions: shock, nightmares, irritability, concentration problems, emotional instability, and physical symptoms. With support from those around them, most officers manage to come to terms with the traumatic event and get on with their lives and careers. (Carlier et al., 1996; Carlier, Lambert & Gersons 1997, 2000).

For those who cannot cope adequately with traumatic events, symptoms of PTSD may become overwhelming. They may become more fearful, aggressive, indifferent, depressed, distracted, or self-absorbed than they were before the traumatic event. Clearly, these changes affect the quality of their lives. In extreme cases, officers might even conclude that life is no longer worth living (Violanti, 2003). The reality of psychological wounds due to workplace trauma has also been one of effects that resulted from 9/11 terrorist attacks and the recent war in Iraq. Since these events, the police and others have been put under additional strain due to personnel shortages in many emergency first-responder occupations as a result of military deployment and homeland security measures (Violanti, 2003). The preceding studies suggest associations among exposure to traumatic work events, PTSD symptomatology, and suicide. We posit in the present study that these factors increase the risk of suicide ideation in police officers that, in turn, may increase the risk of completed suicide.

THE LIFE COURSE MODEL

In its simplest sense, the life course may be viewed as the "duration of a person's existence" (Elder, 1985). Elder (1985) defines the life course as the interconnected trajectories that people have as they go through life. A trajectory is a sequence of linked states within a conceptually defined range of behavior or experience. It is a pathway over the life span. As people move through this trajectory, they graduate from one level to another. Transitions are always embedded in trajectories, and the states that make up a trajectory are always linked to one another by transitions. In sum, there is no such thing as a "static" life, and this holds true for biological, psychological, and social change (Elder, George & Shanahan, 1996).

Examples of Life Course Change

Social and cultural experiences can lead to transitions that change lives. PTSD, a result of traumatic experiences, can certainly be a life course–altering event. Several researchers have suggested that PTSD can pervade through a lifetime. Elder, George, and Shanahan (1996), for example, suggest that contextual features of stress are located temporally within the intersection of personal lives and history. Some examples that integrate life-course themes with stress were war, child abuse, and caregiving.

Elder, Shanahan, and Clipp (1994) examined whether social disruptions resulting from military service entry increased the risk of adverse change in adult health. Apart from preservice factors, the authors found that the late-mobilized men were at greatest risk of negative trajectories on physical health. Worklife disadvantages accounted in part for this health effect. Pathways that link stress and physical decline were discussed as they related to social disruption.

Elder, Gimbel, and Ivie (1991) suggested that military service creates discontinuity in men's lives by removing them from age-graded careers and subjecting them to the dictates of a world in which one's past or life history has no importance. Military service specifically, rather than war generally, was recalled as the life-changing experience. Men were most likely to define past events as turning points when those events had positive effects and were perceived to cause substantial change in their lives.

Wright, Carter, and Cullen (2005) suggested that military service disconnects men from past social and personal disadvantages and thus potentially alters normal life-course patterns of development. Through latent growth curve models, the authors examined the impact of military service in Vietnam on drug use and arrests across the life course. Longitudinal data collected by the Marion County Youth study (1964–

1979) were used to track a sample of men over a fifteen-year period. Analyses of these data revealed substantial nonrandom selection effects associated with service in Vietnam.

Cohan and Cole (2002) examined changes in marriage, birth, and divorce rates following Hurricane Hugo. Time-series analysis indicated that in the year following the hurricane, marriage, birth, and divorce rates increased in the twenty-four counties declared disaster areas compared with the twenty-two other counties in the state. Taken together, the results suggested that a life-threatening event motivated people to take significant action in their close relationships that altered their life course.

THE POLICE CAREER COURSE AND TRAUMA

The association between trauma stress and suicide is likely not a static process. There are events and stages during a police career that may exacerbate this relationship. This chapter proposes a conceptual model describing the impact of traumatic stress through the life course of police officers. A life-course framework first developed by Elder and colleagues (1996) may be a valuable tool to help understand the immediate and long-term effects of trauma exposure on suicide. The usefulness of this approach will depend on seeking out new pathways as well as its ability to explain social, psychological, and temporal patterns of trauma exposure and consequences. This perspective adds to a greater recognition of the mutually interacting connections among trajectories in police trauma and trajectories in other domains of life. Within the framework of this model, we will discuss (1) the impact of preoccupational trauma on officers, (2) assimilation into the police role and the impact of trauma within that role, and (3) the spillover of residual trauma into police retirement.

Similar to military service and deployment disruption, the socialization process of a person from civilian to police officer and back to civilian is a significant life-role transition. An early example of police career transition was suggested by Violanti (1983): (1) A "reality shock" stage, in which the rookie officer realizes that real police work is quite different from what is learned in the academy; (2) a "disenchantment" stage, in which idealistic notions fostered in the police academy become further and further apart from reality; (3) a "personalization" stage, in which the officer begins a renewed emphasis on personal rather than police work goals; and (4) an "introspection" stage, indicative of the senior officer who looks back on early career years as "the good old days."

There are many normative as well as disruptive transition phases within a police career. Phases typically are separated from each other by transitions and tend to be ordered in the sense that certain events are expected to precede or follow other events most of the time. In addition, many transitions and changes can have reciprocal effects on each other (Elder et al., 1996). Figure 3–1 outlines a conceptual model of the police career life course and trauma for the present chapter. An explanation of the model follows.

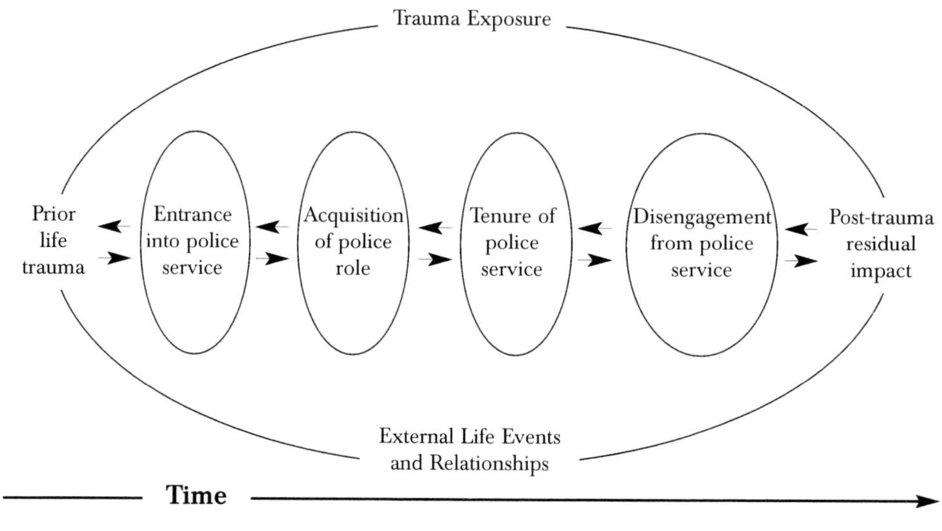

Figure 3–1. Police Career Course Trauma Model.

Preemployment Trauma

Persons who enter police work may come in with emotional baggage. Upon entry to the police academy, officers bring with them a plethora of previous life experiences, both positive and negative (Goldfarb & Aumiller, 2004).This may have a synergistic effect on trauma experienced during the career course of a police officer. Police officers exposed to traumatic events prior to entering their careers have an increased vulnerability to PTSD (Violanti, 1996). Part of this vulnerability may be attributed to a lack of efficacious coping strategies employed by officers to deal with these events (Patterson, 2001). Dependence on the police role as a primary life role may also discourage officers from using other more flexible roles as resources to deal with trauma (Thoits, 1986).

Buchanan, Stephens, and Long (2001) suggest that within those occupations in which exposure to trauma is high previous trauma is an additional risk factor that may have an adverse impact on job performance and resignation. These authors found that the percentage of recruits who reported traumatic events (70.6%) was at the high end of the ranges reported from other samples of younger adults. Burke, Shakespeare-Finch, Paton, and Ryan (2006) investigated the process of adaptation in newly recruited police officers. Highlighted were incidences of difficulty in adjusting to the role of police officer, such as predictors of elevated stress and symptoms of PTSD. Measures of PTSD were higher in recruits who had endured a traumatic incident prior to joining the service compared to recruits who had endured stressful rather than traumatic events.

Thompson and Solomon (1991) found significantly higher levels of PTSD symptomatology in recruits having experienced a prior traumatic life event than in those not experiencing a prior traumatic life event. Huddleston, Paton, and Stephens (2006) point out that high levels of traumatic stress symptoms at point of entry may increase vulnerability to trauma. The manner in which prior trauma interacts with other kinds of experience within the police role may moderate subsequent vulnerability. Factors that could be implicated in this include, for example, access to social support and the capacity to use training and operational experiences to render prior experiences coherent and meaningful.

Becoming a Police Officer

Entry into policing involves a process of abrupt resocialization. A first step in that process is assimilation into the police role (Violanti, 1997a). Assimilation refers to the recruit officer's adaptation to a new work role and appears to occur interactively at individual and social levels. The acquisition process is very strong in initial police training and continues to dominate officers' lives throughout their careers (Harris, 1973).

To the new officer, police work may at first seem exciting and adventurous. Officers can become addicted to their work from what Gilmartin (1990) termed the "brotherhood of biochemistry," a physiological as well as a social dependency on the police role. Gilmartin suggested that the police role created a learned perceptual set that led officers to alter the manner in which they interact with the environment. Officers adapted to excitement and danger, were depressed during calm periods, and became detached from any role unrelated to police work. In his analysis of combat officers, Solursh (1988) found that the combination of mutually excitatory states of danger and recall of such danger led to depression in officers. Van der Kolk (1987) theorized that persons involved in highly stressful jobs may actually become addicted to traumatic exposures. Increased physiological arousal brought about by dangerous or exciting events decreases the individual's ability to assess the nature of current challenges and interferes with rational decision processes.

Unfortunately, officers strongly assimilated to the police role may lack important coping resources such as mental flexibility and supportive relationships (Turvey, 1996). Factors in police work likely to increase the risk of exposure to trauma are danger, shift work, public apathy, a sense of uselessness, and dealing with human misery and death (Spielberger, Westberry, Grier & Greenfield, 1981). Other traumatic events involve shootings, witnessing death and mutilation, disasters, and abused or maltreated children (Violanti & Aron, 1994). Assimilation of officers into the police role also restricts cognitive flexibility, thus impairing their ability to deal with psychological trauma. As a result, the potential for PTSD among exposed police officers may increase.

External Life Course Events

Although repeated exposure to acute work stressors can lead to trauma symptoms, police officers must also deal with stressors external to work. Contending with negative life events (e.g. divorce, serious family or personal illness, and financial difficulties) can affect both the psychological and the physiological well-being of officers as well.

The psychological effects of experiencing life events have been well-studied. Life events often precede depressive episodes and psychiatric disorders such as anxiety states, alcoholism, bulimia, and schizophrenia (Kendler, Karkowski & Prescott, 1998; Kendler, Kessler, Neale, Heath & Eaves, 1993); contribute to depression; and are associated with greater risk of illnesses (Brown & Harris, 1989).

Hartley, Violanti, Fekedulegn, Andrew, and Burchfiel (2007) examined to what extent negative life events and traumatic police incidents are associated with depression in police officers. Among most reported life events were the death of a close relative or friend; decrease in income; and serious arguments with spouse, boss, or coworkers. An increasing stepwise trend in depression scores was observed among officers experiencing a low, medium and high number of negative life events, a finding consistent with work by Paton and colleagues (2003). Experiencing a high number of negative life events over the past year nearly doubled depression scores in this sample of police officers. A stepwise trend was observed among police officers experiencing one or more traumatic incidents over the last year; depression scores increased as the number of incidents experienced increased.

In sum, these studies suggest that police officers who become enmeshed in the exclusiveness of the police role are at a distinct disadvantage when dealing with trauma. Thus, police role assimilation may act as a significant life-course change with respect to mental well-being.

Retirement and Trauma: After the Battle Is Over

Davidson and coworkers (2006) provided preliminary evidence for a phenomenon observed in aging combat veterans termed "late-onset stress symptomatology" (LOSS). LOSS is a phenomenon among older veterans who (1) experienced highly stressful combat events in early adulthood; (2) functioned successfully throughout their lives, with no chronic stress-related disorders; but (3) begin to register increased combat-related thoughts, feelings, reminiscences, memories, or symptoms commensurate with the changes and challenges of aging – sometimes decades after their combat experiences.

Krause, Shaw, and Cairney (2004) evaluated issues regarding the relationship between exposure to trauma over the life course and physical health status in old age. Data from a nationwide survey of older veterans (n = 1518) revealed that trauma was associated with worse health. The data also suggested that trauma experienced between the ages of 18 and 30 years and between the ages of 31 and 64 years had the strongest relationship with poorer health in retirees.

Similar to military service, the life-course impact of police work does not end with retirement or separation from the department (Violanti, 1997b). The exposure of police officers to trauma may be for a period of twenty years or more. With such long-term exposure, officers are still likely to experience symptoms associated with PTSD (Violanti, 1996). For some, PTSD symptomatology may be full blown; for others, a residual condition may exist.

With return to civilian life, police officers take with them emotional baggage remaining from traumatic work experiences. Solomon (1992) suggests that persons who leave traumatic situations tend to generalize avoidance to stimuli resembling the trauma in their new environment. As a result they constrict their scope of activity, social ties, and civilian functioning. This is viewed as a detrimental pattern of residual trauma carried over into the new environment of the separated police officer. The officer's family and close friends may also contribute to this problem by adapting themselves to this widened avoidance.

Police officers spend much of their careers preparing for the worse. Training generally emphasizes the "worst possible case scenario" and prepares officers to deal with that event only. As a result, many officers become occupationally and personally socialized into approaching situations with considerable suspicion. This defensive stance toward life activities can become an obsession and a liability for officers (Gilmartin, 1986). As one result of learned defensiveness, it is not uncommon to find a proportion of what Wilson (1980) refers to as "action junkies;" officers who are addicted to risk behavior. Some officers become addicted to this excitement and cannot function effectively without it when they separate from service.

van der Kolk (1987) states that increased physiological arousal of traumatized persons decreases their ability to assess the nature of current challenges and interferes with the resolution of the trauma. Such persons have difficulty in making calm and rational decisions and tend to rely on instant action rather than on thought. Kolb (1993) hypothesizes that arousal of intense emotional response to traumatic events leads to hypersensitivity and impaired potential for habituation and relearning.

Grigsby (1991) states that "combat rush" is a conditioned emotional response to trauma. Although war is frightening and traumatic, combat may be characterized by periods of intense pleasurable stimulation. These experiences may be reinforcing, leading persons to "seek out" similar trauma. Solursh (1988) views the "rush" experienced by traumatized persons as a response to dullness and boredom in life. They crave excitement as an alternative to a calm lifestyle.

Thus, retiring from police work may not leave officers or their families free of the haunting vestiges of trauma. As a civilian, the officer must learn to adjust to a role that does not involve constant scanning for threats. Therapy may require teaching the officer to learn new reactive patterns. In addition, the wider family consequences of trauma work must be recognized. More research into the implications of repetitive and addictive traumatic stress phenomena is required to augment support and therapeutic strategies.

CONCLUSION

This chapter has presented components of the life course as applied to trauma and police work. The hypotheses proposed here are based on the notion that police exposure to trauma is a mitigating factor in the path to suicide. It is essential to understand that the impact of police work on the mental well-being of officers is not at all a static process but one of continuing and ongoing change. The pathways of such change depend to a great extent on prior, present, and residual exposure. Other things to consider in future work are at what point in the police career the most trauma associated events occurred, where and how they occurred, their intensity and meaning, how peers and the organization responded, and the timeliness and efficacy of intervention or treatment. Perhaps future exploration of the life course model theory presented here can in some small way provide explanations for the track of traumatic stress in police work and, ultimately, solutions on how we may deal with this perplexing problem of suicide.

REFERENCES

American Psychiatric Association. (1994). *Diagnostic and Statistical Manual* (4th ed.). Washington, DC: American Psychological Association.

Brown, G. W., & Harris, T. O. (1989). *Life events and illness.* New York: Guilford.

Buchanan, G., Stephens, C., & Long, N. (2001). Traumatic experiences of new recruits and serving police. *The Australian Journal of Disaster and Trauma Studies.* [Online]. http://trauma.massey.ac.nz/

Burke, K. J., Shakespeare-Finch, J. E., Paton, D., & Ryan, M. (2006). Characterizing the resilient officer: Individual attributes at point of entry to policing. *Traumatology, 12,* 178–188.

Carlier, I. V. E., Fouwels, A. J., Lamberts, R. D., & Gersons, B. P. R. (1996). Posttraumatic stress disorder and dissociation in traumatized police officers. *The American Journal of Psychiatry, 153,* 1325–1328.

Carlier, I. V. E., Lamberts, R. D., & Gersons, B. P. R. (1997). Risk factors for posttraumatic stress in police officers: A prospective analysis. *Journal of Nervous and Mental Disease, 185,* 498–506.

Carlier, I. V. E., Lamberts, R. D., & Gersons, B. P. R. (2000). The dimensionality of trauma: A multidimensional scaling comparison of police officers with and without posttraumatic stress disorder. *Psychiatry Research, 97,* 29–39.

Cohan, C. L., & Cole, S. W. (2002). Life course transitions and natural disaster: Marriage, birth, and divorce following Hurricane Hugo. *Journal of Family Psychology, 6,* 14–25.

Davidson, E. H, Pless, A. P., Gugliucci, M. R., King, L. A., King, D. W., Salgado, D. M., Spiro, A., & Bachrach, P. (2006). Late-life emergence of early-life trauma: The phenomenon of late-onset stress symptomatology among aging combat veterans. *Research on Aging, 28,* 84–114.

Davidson, J., Hughes, D., Blazer, D., & George, L. (1991). Post-traumatic stress disorder in the community: An epidemiological study. *Psychological Medicine, 21,* 713–721.

Dunning, C. (1999). Post intervention strategies to reduce police trauma: A paradigm shift. In J. M. Violanti and D. Paton (Eds.), *Police trauma: Psychological aftermath of civilian combat.* Springfield, IL: Charles C Thomas.

Elder, G. H. (1985). Perspectives on the life course. In G. H. Elder (Ed.), *Life course dynamics* (pp. 23–49). Ithaca, NY: Cornell University Press.

Elder, G. H., George, L. K., & Shanahan, M. J. (1996). Psychosocial stress over the life course. In G. H. Elder (Ed.), *Psychosocial stress: Perspectives on structure, theory, life-course, and methods.* (pp. 247–292). San Diego, CA: Academic Press.

Elder, G. H., Gimbel, C., & Ivie, R. (1991). Turning points in life: The case of military service and war. *Military Psychology, 3,* 215–231.

Elder, G. H., Shanahan, M. J., & Clipp, E. (1994). When war comes to men's lives: Life-course patterns in family, work, and health. *Psychology and Aging, 9,* 5–16.

Farberow, N. L., Kang, H. K., & Bullman, T. (1990). Combat experience and post service psychosocial status as predictors of suicide in Vietnam veterans. *Journal of Nervous and Mental Disease, 178,* 32–37.

Ferrada-Noli, M., Asberg, M., Ormstad, K., Lundin, T., & Sundbom, E. (1998). Suicidal behavior after severe trauma. Part one: PTSD diagnosis, psychiatric comorbidity, and assessments of suicidal behavior. *Journal of Traumatic Stress, 11,* 103–112.

Freeman, T. W., Roca, V., & Moore, W. M. (2000). A comparison of combat related posttraumatic stress disorder patients with and without a history of suicide attempt. *The Journal of Nervous and Mental Disease, 188*, 460–463.

Gilmartin, K. M. (1990).The brotherhood of biochemistry: Its implications for a police career. In H. E. Russel and A. Beigal (Eds.), *Understanding human behavior for effective police work* (pp. 397–418). New York: Basic Books.

Green, B. L., Lindy, J. D., & Grace, M. C. (1989). Multiple diagnosis in posttraumatic stress disorder: The role of war survivors. *Journal of Nervous and Mental Disease, 177*, 329–335.

Harris, R. N. (1973). *The police academy: An inside view.* New York: Wiley.

Hartley, T. A., Violanti, J. M., Fekedulegn, D., Andrew, M. E., & Burchfiel, C. M. (2007). Associations between major life events, traumatic incidents and depression among Buffalo police officers. *International Journal of Emergency Mental Health, 9*, 25–35.

Hendin, H., & Haas, A. (1991). Suicide and guilt as manifestations of PTSD in Vietnam combat veterans. *American Journal of Psychiatry, 148*, 586–591.

Huddleston, L. M., Paton, D., & Stephens, C. (2006). Conceptualizing traumatic stress in police officers: Pre-employment, critical incident, and organizational influences. *Traumatology, 23*, 170–179.

Kendler, K. S., Karkowski, L. M., & Prescott, C. A. (1998). Stressful life events and major depression: Risk period, long-term contextual threat, and diagnostic specificity. *Journal of Nervous and Mental Disease, 86*, 661–669.

Kendler, K. S., Kessler, R. C., Neale, M. C., Heath, A. C., & Eaves, L. J. (1993). The major depression: Risk period, long-term contextual threat, and diagnostic specificity. *Journal of Nervous and Mental Disease, 186*, 661–669.

Kolb, L. C. (1993). The psychobiology of PTSD: Perspectives and reflections of the past, present, and future. *Journal of Traumatic Stress, 6*, 293–304.

Krause, N., Shaw, B. A., & Cairney, J. (2004). A descriptive epidemiology of lifetime trauma and the physical health status of older adults. *Psychology and Aging, 19*, 637–648.

Lehmann, L., McCormick, R., & McCracken, L. (1995). Suicidal behavior among patients in the VA health care system. *Psychiatric Services, 46*, 1069–1071.

Marshall, R. D., Olfson, M., Hellman, F., Blanco, C., & Struening, E. L. (2001). Comorbidity, impairment, and suicidality in subthreshold PTSD. *American Journal of Psychiatry, 158*, 1467–1473.

Paton, D., Violanti, J. M., & Smith, L. M. (2003). *Promoting capabilities to manage post-traumatic stress: Perspectives on resilience.* Springfield, IL: Charles C Thomas.

Patterson, G. T. (2001). The relationship between demographic variables and exposure to traumatic events among police officers. *The Australian Journal of Disaster and Trauma Studies, 2* [Online]. Available: http://trauma.massey.ac.nz/

Roszell, D. K., McFall, M. E., & Malas, K. L. (1991). Frequency of symptoms and concurrent psychiatric disorder in Vietnam veterans with chronic PTSD. *Hospital and Community Psychiatry, 42*, 293–296.

Solomon, Z. (1992). The 'KOACH' project for treatment of combat-related PTSD: Rationale, aims, and methodology. *Journal of Traumatic Stress, 5*, 175–193.

Solursh, L. P. (1988). Combat addiction – PTSD re-explored. *Psychological Journal of the University of Ottawa, 13*, 451–462.
Spielberger, C., Westberry, L., Grier, K., & Greenfield, G. (1981). *The police stress survey: Sources of stress in law enforcement.* Tampa, FL: Human Resources Institute.
Sugimoto, J. D., & Oltjenbruns, K. A. (2001). The environment of death and its influence on police officers in the United States. *Omega, 43*, 145–155.
Thoits, P. A. (1986). Multiple identities: Examining gender and marital differences in distress. *American Sociological Review, 51*, 259–272.
Thompson, J., & Solomon, M. (1991). Body recovery teams at disasters: Trauma or challenge? *Anxiety Research, 4*, 235–240.
Turvey, B. (1996). *Police officers: Control, hopelessness, and suicide* [Online]. Available: http://www.connix.com
van der Kolk, B. A. (1987). *Psychological trauma.* Washington, DC: American Psychiatric Press.
Violanti, J. M. (1983). Stress patterns in police work: A longitudinal study. *Journal of Police Science and Administration, 11*, 211–216.
Violanti, J. M. (1996). Traumatic stress and police work. In D. Paton and J. M. Violanti (Eds.), *Traumatic stress in critical occupations: Recognition, treatment and consequences* (pp. 87–107). Springfield, IL: Charles C Thomas.
Violanti, J. M. (1997a). Suicide and the police role: A psychosocial model. *Policing: An International Journal of Police Strategy and Management, 20*, 698–715.
Violanti, J. M. (1997b). Residuals of police occupational trauma. *The Australian Journal of Disaster and Trauma Studies, 3* [Online]. Available: http://trauma.massey.ac.nz/
Violanti, J. M. (2003). Suicide and the police culture. In D. Hackett and J. M. Violanti (Eds.), *Police suicide: Tactics for prevention.* Springfield, IL: Charles C Thomas.
Violanti, J. M., & Aron, F. (1994). Ranking police stressors. *Psychological Reports, 75*, 824–826.
Wilson, J. P. (1980). Conflict, stress and growth: The effects of the Vietnam war on psychological development of Vietnam veterans. In C. R. Figley & S. Leventman (Eds.), *Strangers at home: Vietnam veterans since the war.* New York: Praeger.
Wright, J. P., Carter, D. E., & Cullen, F. T. (2005). A life-course analysis of military service in Vietnam. *Journal of Research in Crime and Delinquency, 42*, 55–83.

Chapter 4

WHY POLICE OFFICERS *DO NOT* COMMIT SUICIDE: PERSONAL AND ORGANIZATIONAL RESILIENCY

JOHN M. VIOLANTI

INTRODUCTION

We accept the notion that exposure to trauma may be a mitigating factor in police suicide. Despite exposure to traumatic incidents and the tragedy of suicide, however, the fact remains that the majority of officers cope well enough with police work to survive their careers. Are there protective factors that help officers cope with the stresses, strains, and trauma of police work? If there are such forces at work, it is important to describe them. The concept of resiliency may fulfill such a role and, in doing so, may provide the necessary prevention mechanism required to psychologically survive a police career.

Following Antonovsky's (1990) definition, resilience reflects the extent to which individuals and groups can call upon their psychological and physical resources and competencies in ways that allow them to render challenging events coherent, manageable, and meaningful. In this sense, resiliency refers not only to personality factors but also to the police social milieu, including the organization. We term this combination the "police stress shield" resilience model (Paton et al., 2008).

It is also important to consider the common meaning of resiliency. Resilience is often used to imply an ability to bounce back. Being able to bounce back is an important ability. Because police officers are *repeatedly* called upon to deal with increasingly complex and threatening incidents, however, it is appropriate to expand the scope of this definition to include the development of one's capacity to deal with *future* events (Paton, Smith, Violanti & Eranen, 2000). Therefore, resilience can provide support not only in the here and now but also in the future. This is the notion of "adaptive capacity" (Klein, Nicholls & Thomalla, 2003). Police resiliency therefore includes the capacity of agencies and officers to draw on individual, collective, and institutional resources to cope with demands, challenges, and changes encountered *during and after* critical incidents.

PERSONAL RESILIENCY

Hardiness

A growing body of literature shows that persons with high levels of hardiness – marked by a strong sense of commitment, control, and challenge – tend to remain healthy under stress compared to those low in hardiness. (Kobasa, 1979; Solomon, Mikulincer & Hobfoll, 1986; Bartone, Ursano, Wright & Ingraham, 1989; King, King, Fairbank, Keane, & Adams, 1998; Maddi, 1999). Hardiness can be thought of as a personality style or tendency, reasonably stable over time and across situations, that somehow confers resiliency on those who possess it. A critical aspect of the hardiness resiliency mechanism probably involves the interpretations, or the meanings, that people attach to events around them, as well as to their own place in the world of experiences. Highly hardy people will typically interpret experience as (1) interesting and worthwhile overall; (2) something they can exert control over; and (3) challenging, presenting opportunities to learn and grow. Maddi (2001) conceives of hardiness as a generalized personality style.

The ability of hardiness to buffer or transform stressful experiences seems to be related to the particular interpretations of such experiences typically made by the hardy person. If a stressful or painful experience can be framed and made sense of within a broader perspective that holds that all of existence is essentially interesting, worthwhile, a matter of one's own choice, and a chance to learn and grow, then the stressful experience can have beneficial psychological effects rather than harmful ones (Bartone & Adler, 1999).

Recent research findings lend support to the notion that hardiness can be increased in individuals. For example, using a structured intervention program, Maddi (1987) successfully increased hardiness levels in corporate managers and at the same time found that their physiological responses to stress were attenuated and healthier. Maddi and colleagues have followed up this work with a more refined "hardiness induction" program that appears to work quite well (Maddi, Khoshaba & Pammenter, 1999). A key feature of hardiness training involves facilitating the adoption and application of new strategies for interpreting and making sense of experiences, especially highly stressful ones.

Posttraumatic Growth

There are some people who experience a sense of growth from trauma. They may feel that they have learned from the experience and it has made them a better person. Such people may be more resistant to depression and less likely to consider trauma-related suicide. Tedeschi and Calhoun (1995) term this "posttraumatic growth." Posttraumatic growth is defined as a significant beneficial change in cognitive and emotional life beyond previous levels of adaptation, psychological functioning, or life awareness. These changes happen in the aftermath of psychological traumas that challenge previously existing assumptions about self, others, and the future (Calhoun & Tedeschi, 1999; Tedeschi & Calhoun, 1995; Tedeschi, Park & Calhoun, 1998). Trauma-related life changes include greater appreciation of life; warmer, more intimate relationships with others; a greater sense of personal strength; recognition of new possibilities or paths for one's life; and spiritual development (Tedeschi, Park & Calhoun, 1998).

Posttraumatic growth is considered distinct from resilience. Resilience is usually considered to be an ability to bounce back from life difficulties, whereas posttraumatic growth refers to a change in people that goes *beyond* a return to previous functioning and involves a movement beyond pretrauma levels of adaptation. However, according to Tedeschi and Calhoun (1995), although posttraumatic growth is distinct, there is likely some connection between posttraumatic growth and resilience, as well as concepts such as sense of coherence and hardiness.

Social support may play a strong role in the development of posttraumatic growth when it involves mutual disclosure or mutual help, and the absence of such support and disclosure can have the opposite effect. Cordova, Cunningham, Carlson, and Andrykowski (in press) reported that in breast cancer survivors who found that friends and family did not wish to hear about their illness, cognitive processing appeared to be inhibited. The less cognitive processing there was, the less posttraumatic growth was reported by the survivors. Our perspective on this can be summed up by stating that perhaps the greatest benefit of therapy in groups for posttraumatic growth is the discussion of perspective, offering of beliefs, and use of metaphor to explain experience. All of this is fertile ground for the revision of schemas that is essential to the experience of growth (Calhoun & Tedeschi, 1999, p. 68).

ORGANIZATIONAL RESILIENCY

Although typically investigated at the personality level of the individual, the comprehensive understanding of resilience must also integrate organizational perspectives, with the police organization perhaps exerting a greater influence in this process. The police organization defines the context within which officers experience and interpret critical incidents and their sequelae and within which future capabilities are nurtured or restricted (Paton, 2006). There are three characteristics of a resilient organization to consider: (1) organizational climate, (2) trust, and (3) leadership.

Organizational Climate

Hart and Cooper (2001) proposed a conceptual model of organizational climate that predicts salutary outcomes. Organizational climate describes officers' perceptions of how their organization functions, and these perceptions influence both their well-being and their performance in their organizational role (Hart & Cooper, 2001). Burke and Paton (2006) tested the ability of this model to predict satisfaction in the context of emergency responders' experience of critical incidents. Organizational climate was the best single predictor of job satisfaction and represents a significant influence on officers' ability to render their critical incident experiences meaningful and manageable. Organizational climate had a direct positive influence on coping, resulting in an increase in positive work experiences. Organizational climate also demonstrated a direct negative influence on negative work experiences. The important role played by organizational climate indicates that police agencies have a key role in facilitating officer adaptability and resilience.

Trust

Police officers are noted for not trusting. This may be a result of occupational socialization, which emphasizes that trusting can put one in danger on the street. Instead, it is "safe" to be suspicious of everyone. Unfortunately, this lack of trust may impede the officer's ability to seek help in stressful situations. Trust is a prominent determinant of the effectiveness of interpersonal relationships, group processes, and organizational relationships (Barker & Camarata, 1998; Herriot, Hirch & Reilly, 1998) and plays a crucial role in empowering officers (Spreitzer & Mishra, 1999). People functioning in trusting, reciprocal relationships are left feeling empowered and are more likely to experience meaning in their work. Trust has been identified as a predictor of people's ability to deal with complex, high-risk events (Siegrist & Cvetkovich, 2000), particularly when relying on others to provide information or assistance.

An officer contemplating suicide does not trust. This is especially true regarding the organization. The resilient organization is one where the officer can go for help without reprise or hesitation. An officer is more willing to commit to acting cooperatively in high-risk situations when he or she believes those with whom they must collaborate or work are competent, dependable, and likely to act with integrity and to care for their interests (Dirks, 1999). Organizations functioning with cultures that value openness and trust create opportunities for officers to engage in learning and growth, contributing to the development of officers' adaptive capacity (Barker & Camarata, 1998).

Leadership

Resilient police organizations have leaders who care about their people. For the suicidal officer, a leader can be the first step to getting help. Leaders play a central role in developing and sustaining empowering environments (Liden, Wayne & Sparrow, 2000; Paton & Stephens, 1996). They have a major role to play in creating and sustaining a climate of trust as a result of their being responsible for translating organizational culture into the day-to-day values and procedures that sustain officers. Leadership practices such as positive reinforcement help create an empowering work environment (Paton, 1994).

Leaders are in a unique position to shape how members of the group understand stressful experiences. The leader who, through example and discussion, communicates a positive construction or reconstruction of shared stressful experiences may exert an influence on the entire group in the direction of his or her interpretation of the experience. Thus, leaders who have a high level of hardiness will likely have a greater impact on their groups under high-stress conditions, when by their example as well as explanations they articulate to group members (including interpretive stories and parables) and encourage an interpretation of stressful events as interesting challenges that group members are capable of meeting and, in any event, can learn and benefit from. This process itself, as well as the positive result of the process (a shared understanding of the event as something worthwhile and beneficial), could be expected to also generate an increased sense of shared values, mutual respect, and cohesion (Bartone & Snook, 1999).

Supportive supervision is a crucial factor (Liden, Sparrow & Wayne, 1997) because it enhances the resiliency necessary for the feelings of competence. Support enables officers to find increased meaning in their work and perhaps their lives. In times of crisis, supervisory support can make the difference between life and death. Focusing on constructive discussion of work-related problems and how they can be resolved draws away from one's personal and psychological weaknesses in difficult situations and replaces them with an active approach to anticipating how to exercise control (Paton & Stephens, 1996). This can be valuable for suicide prevention efforts.

Police managers need to "walk the talk" by communicating to workers a reaction and assessment that reinforces comprehensibility, manageability, and meaningfulness regarding their performance in the event within the context of the organization. They need to be especially cognizant of the profound effect their words and actions can have on workers. Unintended negative consequences can be harder to address and more long lasting and devastating than the traumatic event itself. Cohen and Welch (2000) underscore the ability of the attitudes, beliefs, values, and culture of the organization and its members to mediate the effects of stress and trauma. Administrators must be aware of the messages they send that undercut workers' beliefs regarding their role in prevention, protection, intervention, mitigation, remediation, investigation, and resolution. Coworkers and peers, supervisors, and mental health caregivers must no longer ignore the importance of sociocultural context and group norms (Dunning, 2003).

CONCLUSION

Resilience is not just a personality trait. It is most effective when applied to the total police environment, which includes the organization. Resilient police organizational climates can help to reduce the psychological strain on officers as well as provide a "place to go to" in crisis situations, especially in cases of potential suicide. The police stress shield model describes resilience as resulting from the interaction between personal organizational factors. However, the benefit of any model is a function of its being theoretically rigorous and capable of informing the design practical programs in police organizations. Guidelines for changing hardiness, peer support, supervisor support, and organizational trust are available in the literature (Bartone, 2004; Cogliser & Schriesheim, 2000; Hart et al., 1993; Herriot et al., 1998; Perry, 1997; Quinn & Spreitzer, 1997).

REFERENCES

Antonovsky, A. (1990). Personality and health: Testing the sense of coherence model. In H. S. Friedman (Ed.), *Personality and disease* (pp. 155–177). New York: John Wiley & Sons.

Barker, R. T., & Camarata, M. R. (1998).The role of communication in creating and maintaining a learning organization: Preconditions, indicators, and disciplines. *The Journal of Business Communication, 35*, 443–467.

Bartone, P. (2004). Increasing resiliency through shared sensemaking: Building hardiness in groups. In D. Paton, J. Violanti, C. Dunning, & L. M. Smith (Eds.), *Managing traumatic stress risk: A proactive approach.* Springfield, IL: Charles C Thomas.

Bartone, P. T., & Adler, A. B. (1999). Cohesion over time in a medical peacekeeping task force. *Military Psychology, 11*, 85–107.

Bartone, P. T., & Snook, S. A. (May, 1999). *Cognitive and personality factors predict leader development in U.S. Army cadets.* Paper presented at the 35th International Applied Military Psychology Symposium (IAMPS), Florence, Italy.

Bartone, P. T., Ursano, R. J., Wright, K. W., & Ingraham, L. H. (1989). The impact of a military air disaster on the health of assistance workers: A prospective study. *Journal of Nervous and Mental Disease, 177*, 317–328.

Burke, K., & Paton, D. (2006). Well-being in protective services personnel: Organizational influences. *Australian Journal of Disaster and Trauma Studies, 2006-2* [Online]. http://trauma.massey.ac.nz/issues/2006-2/burke.htm

Calhoun, L. G., & Tedeschi, R. G. (1999). *Facilitating posttraumatic growth: A clinician's guide.* Mahwah, NJ: Lawrence Erlbaum Associates.

Cogliser, C. C., & Schriesheim, C. A. (2000). Exploring work unit context and leader-member exchange: A multi-level perspective. *Journal of Organizational Behavior, 21*, 487–511.

Cohen, J., & Welch, L. (2000). Attitudes, beliefs, values, cultures as mediators of stress. In V. Rice (Ed.), *Handbook of stress, coping and health.* Thousand Oaks, CA: Sage.

Cordova, M. J., Cunningham, L. L. C., Carlson, C. R., & Andrykowski, M. A. (2001). Posttraumatic growth following breast cancer: A controlled comparison study. *Health Psychology, 20*, 176–185.

Dirks, K. T. (1999). The effects of interpersonal trust on work group performance. *Journal of Applied Psychology, 84*, 445–455.

Dunning, C. (2003). Sense of coherence in managing trauma workers. In D. Paton, J. M. Violanti, and L. M. Smith (Eds.), *Promoting capabilities to manage posttraumatic stress: Perspectives on resilience.* Springfield, IL: Charles C Thomas.

Hart, P. M., & Cooper, C. L. (2001). Occupational stress: Toward a more integrated framework. In N. Anderson, D. S. Ones, H. K. Sinangil, and C. Viswesvaren (Eds.), *Handbook of industrial, work and organizational psychology* (vol. 2). London: Sage.

Hart, P. M., & Cooper, C. L. (2001). Occupational Stress: Toward a more integrated framework. In N. Anderson, D. S. Ones, H. K. Sinangil, & C. Viswesvaren (Eds.), *International handbook of work and organizational psychology* (vol. 2). London: Sage.

Herriot, P., Hirsh, W., & Reilly, P. (1998). *Trust and transition: Managing today's employment relationship.* New York: John Wiley & Sons.

King, L., King, D., Fairbank, J., Keane, T., & Adams, G. (1998). Resilience-recovery factors in post-traumatic stress disorder among male and female Vietnam veterans: Hardiness, postwar social support, and additional stressful life events. *Journal of Personality and Social Psychology, 74*, 420–434.

Klein, R., Nicholls, R., & Thomalla, F. (2003). Resilience to natural hazards: How useful is this concept? *Environmental Hazards, 5*, 35–45.

Kobasa, S. C. (1979). Stressful life events, personality, and health: An inquiry into hardiness. *Journal of Personality and Social Psychology, 37*, 1–11.

Liden, R. C., Wayne, S. J., & Sparrow, R. T. (2000). An examination of the mediating role of psychological empowerment on the relations between the job, interpersonal relationships, and work outcomes. *Journal of Applied Psychology, 85,* 407–416.

Maddi, S. R. (1999). The personality construct of hardiness: Effects on experiencing, coping and strain. *Consulting Psychology Journal, 51,* 83–94.

Maddi, S. R. (1987). Hardiness training at Illinois Bell Telephone. In J. P. Opatz (Ed.), *Health promotion evaluation.* Stephens Point, WI: National Wellness Institute.

Maddi, S. R., Khoshaba, D. M., & Pammenter, A. (1999). The hardy organization: Success by turning change to advantage. *Consulting Psychology Journal, 51,* 117–124.

Paton, D. (1994). Disaster relief work: An assessment of training effectiveness. *Journal of Traumatic Stress, 7,* 275–288.

Paton, D. (2006). Posttraumatic growth in emergency professionals. In L. Calhoun and R. Tedeschi (Eds.), *Handbook of posttraumatic growth: Research and practice.* Mahwah, NJ: Lawrence Erlbaum Assoc.

Paton, D., Smith, L. M., Violanti, J., & Eranen, L. (2000). Work-related traumatic stress: Risk, vulnerability and resilience. In D. Paton, J. M. Violanti, and C. Dunning (Eds.), *Posttraumatic stress intervention: Challenges, issues and perspectives* (pp. 187–204). Springfield, IL: Charles C Thomas.

Paton, D., & Stephens, C. (1996). Training and support for emergency responders. In D. Paton and J. Violanti (Eds.), *Traumatic stress in critical occupations: Recognition, consequences and treatment.* Springfield, IL: Charles C Thomas.

Paton, D., Violanti, J. M., Johnston, P., Burke, K., Clarke. J., & Keenan, D. (2008). Stress shield: A model of police resiliency. *International Journal of Emergency Mental Health, 10,* 95–107.

Perry, I. (1997). Creating and empowering effective work teams. *Management Services, 41,* 8–11.

Quinn, R. E., & Spreitzer, G. M. (1997). The road to empowerment: Seven questions every leader should consider. *Organizational Dynamics, Autumn,* 37–49.

Solomon, Z., Mikulincer, M., & Hobfoll, S. E. (1986). Effects of social support and battle intensity on loneliness and breakdown during combat. *Journal of Personality and Social Psychology, 51,* 1269–1276.

Spreitzer, G. M., & Mishra, A. K. (1999). Giving up control without losing control: Trust and its substitutes' effect on managers involving employees in decision making. *Group & Organization Management, 24,* 155–187.

Tedeschi, R. G., & Calhoun, L. G. (1995). *Trauma and transformation: Growing in the aftermath of suffering.* Thousand Oaks, CA: Sage.

Tedeschi, R. G., Park, C. L., & Calhoun, L. G. (Eds.). (1998). *Posttraumatic growth: Positive changes in the aftermath of crisis.* Mahwah, NJ: Lawrence Erlbaum.

Chapter 5

THE REALITY OF SUICIDE: TO THE EDGE AND BACK

Andrew F. O'Hara

An undercover detective, after seeing his partner executed, begged for mercy before being killed himself in a weapons-buying sting gone awry, a prosecutor said Monday in closing arguments at the alleged gunman's death penalty trial.

Pleading for his life, begging to live, knowing he would never see his family again, knowing that this was the end – that, ladies and gentlemen, is how this officer spent his last moments on this earth, the prosecutor told jurors in federal court.

Associated Press

The story I am about to share with you has taken me many years to tell. I have been afraid to tell it – afraid of you, your judgment, and your condemnation. Even today it makes me nervous.

Especially if you're a cop. I spent most of my twenty-four–year career as a California Highway Patrolman hiding this story. It was all wrapped up in the nightmare of a single day in which I was overwhelmed and almost murdered with my own gun. It was one of several "dirty little secrets" I would carry alone until my career ended with a near suicide. I guarded it closely. Only after lengthy therapy was I able to tell my tale in one piece without gagging or crying.

I have learned over the years and in talking to countless other officers that these "dirty little secrets" aren't all that uncommon. In fact, I learned that most cops who have been out there in the arena, doing the dirty work, have them. Perhaps they do not evoke the same feelings of hurt, anger, embarrassment, or, worse, shame. But, big or small, they can lurk, flirt with the mind, hide and play with your dreams, and never really show themselves until they gang together in one big pile of "crap" and come at you like a rotten bunch of little demons.

So what do they look like? They are all the things that "aren't heroic." They are the mistakes, which do happen over the years and decades if you are in the middle of things and making the decisions – if you are a cop, you can't help but make the mistakes. They are the things that go wrong when you've done everything *right* – and you end up on the carpet. Old timers know "cop-gremlins" make it happen, but you cannot tell the lieutenant that because he'll retire you out before you're finished getting crazy. So you sign the paper and keep going. You keep your mouth shut whenever you can and keep an eye out behind you. Cops who are still enamored with themselves and have not gotten over the boast that they never make mistakes or that the mistakes never bother them are doomed to never learn – worse, to never grow. They get to be rookies for life.

Often, the "secrets" are just stupid little things. Some you do not talk about because they would embarrass the hell out of you. Some you do not share because they almost got you killed and stupidity was the only thing that saved you.

Give me a bullet wound, a knife wound, a scar – I have wanted to scream. *Let me tear open my shirt and say, "Here is my wound – look, this is the mark of my tragedy! Touch it, feel it, and know that it still brings me pain!"* People with PTSD cannot do that. When they tear open their shirts, their wounds and scars are invisible. They walk invisibly through a crowd. They drive their patrol units and answer their calls day after day, night after night, holding the pieces together, sometimes until retirement or, sometimes, until the glass shatters. Some will kill themselves.

Each year, there are between 130 and 150 police suicides. We estimate that for each police suicide there are as many as 1,000 officers who continue working while suffering from anxiety disorders, depression, and other clinical manifestations of job stress and trauma.

In some ways, a cop's work may be even more traumatic than that of a soldier sent into a war zone. Anderson and Dahlgren (2002) write, "The police officer's job, over many years, exposes and reexposes them to traumatic events that would make anybody recoil in horror."

Critical incidents, such as shootings, child deaths, and particularly gruesome accidents, are terrible experiences. The positive side of a critical incident, however, is that an increasing number of departments have learned to recognize and react to them with Critical Incident Response Debriefings and teams designed to lessen the emotional impact on involved officers.

That does not happen with cumulative traumas. They build up like bumblebee stings. One sting can be bearable, but as the number of stings increases, they become more of a problem until they become life threatening. Same thing when it comes to these "little incidents." Not only are the events that contribute to cumulative PTSD difficult for supervisors to recognize, but they are hard for the officer as well. A cop might just brush the incidents off as "uncomfortable," unpleasant, or easy to forget. Untrained at monitoring their own physiological and emotional alarm signals, officers miss them, shove them down, ignore them, drink them away, or pick any of a dozen "maladaptive behaviors" to survive and keep on going.

The result is that thousands of officers go through their careers not realizing that they have been emotionally battered and wounded by decades in an occupation known for its hostility, betrayal, carnage, and horror.

I kept my own tale tightly sealed in my memory, hidden from everyone (and myself) for almost twenty years. As time passed, I added the deaths of two fellow officers, horrific accidents, assaults, the bitter betrayal of a high-ranking commander, and the screams and lifeless eyes of far too many human beings. I survived – not as a hero, warrior, paladin, centurion, Lancelot or knight in Kevlar – but as a simple peace officer who did his duty the only way he knew how.

This story ends with a failure, one I am proud of – my attempted suicide. Why? Because from it I gained purpose in life. It took a long recovery after I flirted with my own gun to find that there is no such thing as "no hope." I have learned that from the many cops and firefighters I have had the honor and privilege to talk to and work with in their recovery from trauma.

Those of us who have walked on that dark side of law enforcement, the side of trauma, darkness and isolation, realize that there was a lot we could have done to avoid turning down that path. We also realize there were no road signs to keep us going in the right direction. As the forest got deeper and darker, we could no longer hear the voices warning us to be careful and to get help. We knew we were not supposed to need help. As cops, we waited until it was too late.

For most of the years that I was a cop, I was a long distance runner. Regardless of the shift I worked, I ran several miles a day. I wish that, early in my career, someone had told me that my emotional well-being, my mental health, was just as important as my physical health and prowess with a gun. I knew I was not supposed to kill myself. Psychologists had come to our office and told us that. No one told me, though, how I was supposed to take care of myself and my mind, especially as a cop. How does one get through twenty or thirty years of this without going crazy?

Before I knew it, I was at the cliff, ready to jump.
If only I'd known. By reading this, maybe you will.

Police technology has advanced tremendously since the 1960s and 1970s. During a time in my career when I was working a rural area as a highway patrolman, our personal protective equipment was limited to a pine stick with a rubber grommet and a revolver. There were no portable radios. You had a Motorola between the front seats with a microphone cord that reached to the door. At an accident, officers would run down an embankment to check the injuries, clamber back up and grab the mike to order ambulances and tow trucks, then run back down to the victims. Each time the dispatcher or another unit called on the car's outside speaker, the cop would run back and forth.

On a traffic stop, your initial evaluation was important because, when you made the approach, you were divorcing yourself from all communication with the outside world. Once away from the car, you took care of yourself or hoped you could get back to the patrol car in a hurry. Smart officers rolled the passenger window down and tossed the microphone over the spotlight handle for quick access. The rest of police work has not changed a bit since then, however. Safety and alertness are just as important as they were thirty-five years ago.

One pleasant spring day in the hills, however, I was sloppy. On a little-traveled road, I came through a curve and found an older model car that had slid into the ditch parallel to the pavement. There was no other damage and it was not a hazard. The license plate was clear in the system, so I drove on.

It was only a short distance before I caught up with a man walking away from the car. Tapping the horn, I stopped a short distance behind him and stepped out of the car. He stopped, turned and looked at me. Medium height, the thirty-something–year-old was stocky and had broad shoulders. I figured my casual manner gave him no cause for alarm. I was wrong. When I asked for his identification, he backed up and started to turn away. Without thinking, I stepped right into him and grabbed him by the shoulder, saying, "Whoa, whoa there."

The air was knocked out of me as he charged right into me, pushing me backwards. As I backpedaled, I lost my footing and we both tumbled down into the ditch. I fell flat on my back in a coil of barbed wire, with him right on top of me. This happened to be the final section of a fence and loose coils of leftover wire spindled loosely around on the ground. The coils began snaking up around me as I tried to kick my assailant off. I had my handcuffs in one hand, but my arms were blocked by his body and arms. He was all over me, his legs straddling mine. I could not feel the wire barbs, even though they were tearing through my uniform and into my arms. As I struggled, I realized he was going for my gun.

The holster I had was a type they called a "breakfront," which opened all the way down the front. It was held together by a snap, and there was a particular maneuver one used to pull it out. None of this mattered – in his frenzy, the suspect seemed determined to rip my entire gun belt off if he needed to. I was starting to panic as I tried twisting, pushing his arms away and punching at him in short jabs. The barbed wire tore at my shirt as I did. He was determined and had one desperate purpose in mind. He wanted to get away, and he would kill me to do it.

> *I hoped I was right. So I begged. I begged for my life. I put my hands in the air, palms up, and pleaded, Please, let me go. I will not bother you. I will not come after you. Please.*

He froze. For whatever was going on in his mind or whatever he was afraid of, we "connected" in that instant. He sat back and looked at me, almost surprised. Quickly, he jumped off me, out of the wire and over into the field. After several steps, he turned around and looked back, perhaps fearful that I would try to follow or shoot at him. I did not do either. I watched as he ran off into the trees.

Picking myself loose from the wire, I stood and staggered up to the roadway. My first thought was relief that there were no cars or people around. Next, I felt a wave of dizziness and nausea and staggered to the patrol car. I got in and sat, waiting for my head to clear and trying to focus my eyes and thoughts. Checking the volume on the radio, I noticed my fingers were numb. I checked the time on my watch and it did not make sense. I remembered it was afternoon. It scared me to be disoriented. After some deep breaths, I collected myself. I took some back roads to my home, changed uniforms and cleaned up, and went back to my beat. Somehow, I finished out my shift.

I never reported this incident. For days, I tried to fight away any memory of the incident. I walked, I ran, I panicked, and my mind whirled. In short time, I found that alcohol helped tremendously. A moderate drinker before, I began to drink heavily. Beer, hard liquor, or a mix of the two helped the process of "forgetting." Soon the habit became an addiction – a vicious one. When my shift ended, a couple of warm beers under the car seat were enough to get me home to a twelve-pack of cold ones in the refrigerator.

Booze was a mighty and wonderful friend when it came to stress and memories, and in those days "Choir Practice" was still popular. Five or six of us would gather on a dark frontage road in the dark, summer and winter, drinking and roaring jokes. A couple of hours of this was only a beginning for me. At home, I would drink at the television into the early morning hours, making sure I was solidly drunk before staggering to bed.

I ruined a marriage and raised two sons as a drunk, but the alcohol remained my best partner for eleven years. I was what they call a "high functioning alcoholic." I carefully timed my drinking so that I could report for the next shift without an odor on my breath (or so I thought). I was always sharp in appearance and rarely called in sick. In retrospect, I have little doubt that most of my peers knew I was a drunk.

A few months into my second marriage, I found myself facing the choice of another divorce or giving up the drinking. I had humiliated myself in enough places and found myself in so many gutters by that time – without endangering my job, miraculously – that I was able, after eleven years of stuporous drinking and a couple of attempts, to quit.

That's when my real problems began. Without the protection of my booze, I was at the mercy of my demons. All the little cop-gremlins, my memories, were free to play. Not that they all came at once. At first there was the struggle and uncertainty of my initial sobriety and the gradual adjustment, mentally and physically, to a new lifestyle without chemical addiction. My biggest revelation, however, was learning that sobriety means an entirely new way of thinking. You cannot have one without the other, and you might as well die if you do not have both.

It wasn't long before the demons started coming out of the closet. The first to come visit me was the man in the ditch. He started dropping by more and more frequently, often in my dreams and then more and more in my waking thoughts. He would laugh at me – laugh and call me "coward." I thought I had forgotten him, back in the haze of the alcohol, but the brain remembers *everything*, storing it until the dam overflows. In law enforcement, this happens all too easily.

> The Buick Riviera, I wrote in my journal, suddenly brakes down from 110 mph and swerves across the freeway, bouncing onto the off-ramp. I barely squeeze off after him. It gives me a chance to close the distance. My foot is to the floor of my Dodge as I dog him down the two-lane highway. For once, traffic is pulling over neatly and my teeth are set, watching his head bob back and forth in the rear view mirror as he watches me. Suddenly, he throws his car left into a violent U-turn through a small, rural gas station and tries to loop back through the pumps. I damn near whoop because I'm far enough behind that I can cut him off and I do just that, plowing straight into his driver's door as hard as I can as he tries to squeeze past me. My wheels are squealing smoke as I shove him sideways, back against a fence. His eyes are saucers as I bail and level my gun across the hood and scream at him to freeze, almost hoping he won't.
>
> He has no identification and I can't find any registration. I try running the plates, but the dispatcher tells me the system is down. I search the car and finally I look at a nice, shiny briefcase on the seat. Seems like a logical place to look for identification and registration. There wasn't any. But there was what looked to me like a million dollars worth of powdered cocaine, neatly packed in cellophane bags. The judge threw it all out as a bad search, but at least my hotshot driver only got an empty briefcase back.

Few cops keep diaries or journals. I began as a part of my therapy. It helped me reconstruct (and deal with) many of the things that bothered me. It also helped me (finally) remember some of the things I did well and of which I was proud. Oddly, after retiring, I was able to list dozens of "negatives" about my career and only a few "positives." I was ready to give up finding more but, at the urging of my therapist and a long, frustrating struggle, I finally came up with a lengthy and gratifying list. Oh, there are those "Old Salts" who convert every memory, no matter how horrible, into a heroic or humorous sea story that gets better with every year. I envy them – I'm one of those who can only remember events as they actually occurred. Like screams.

As of this writing, I'm still careful about watching television or certain movies because screams will trigger me immediately. I've had to get up and leave theaters or living rooms abruptly because of them. To this day, I choose not have a television set.

> I receive the call of a double homicide on the outskirts of town. It's a run-down house, I remember, and the report is that the suspect has fled up into the hills. An old man is gesturing frantically from the roadside. I turn around and pull into the property as he runs to the door of the home and points inside, excitedly. I can't understand a word he's saying. Several other units arrive and we surround and then enter the house, where we find a young couple sitting on the floor, against the wall, staring at us. Standing there, gun in hand, I look into their faces. A man in his mid-twenties and a very pretty young girl, both are staring at me quite peacefully. Both have bullet holes in their foreheads. Neatly and perfectly placed, I think to myself. There was no fight. Did they scream? Their last living sight was of their executioner, one at a time. Were they staring at me, now? No time to wonder – I turn my mind back to the suspect. Is he . . . With a start, I sense a deputy standing beside me, also staring. He must be having similar thoughts. We look at one another, shake it off, and head for the back door to join the search for the suspect.

ON THE EDGE – THE PATH TO SUICIDE

I didn't just wake up one morning with PTSD. Nor did I walk into the psychiatrist's office and walk out with an immediate diagnosis of PTSD. It's a gathering storm. For example, in one of my early journal entries, I wrote:

> May 3. Tired tired tired!!! Nervous, gears spinning and going nowhere. Suspicious. Hardly any sleep. Talked to Captain and Lieutenant today, they understand things are tough. Both were supportive (weren't they?). I've been seeing a therapist for a month now, and have started on anti-depressants with no noticeable effect, yet. All of it's been very confusing for me. In all my years of law enforcement, I've never paid any attention to this business of stress – I've never

heard of posttraumatic stress disorder, either, and I'm still having difficulty understanding it.

Things have begun happening to me that are scaring me, but I'm not telling anyone. Bit by bit, I'm sharing some of it with my therapist. I'm having nightmares about terrible things and I'm waking up in the middle of the night. Then I can't go back to sleep, which is starting to affect me. What really bothers me is that I'm getting increasingly irritable, snapping at people at work and shouting at my family without provocation. That's not "me," and it just makes me more anxious.

It's truly frightening to realize that things are "happening in your mind" and that you have no control over them. This is why, once a diagnosis of PTSD is made, it is important that the patient understand that it's a disorder that depends on a factor *outside the individual* and that a diagnosis of PTSD is not even possible unless there has been exposure to a traumatic experience. There has to be an event that caused it.

The path to my collapse was slow – in that it didn't happen overnight. Ultimately, it took place over many months as I struggled with all my might to hang onto myself and my job. For me, it was one personal, tragic event for which I took personal blame (needlessly, as I would find out, later) that finally triggered the end.

We needed someone to work overtime until early morning, and Duane is always the first to volunteer. When he shows up in the sergeant's office, he looks tired. He's worked at least four nights in a row of overtime and his eyes are red.

"Come on, guy," I kid, "you're tired! You've worked enough this week. Go on home and get some sleep and maybe take the next offer."

"Aw, sarge, you worry too much, man! I've never been turned down. Besides, I go home and spend all my time sleeping, so I'm always in good shape when I come in."

"Don't give me that crap, Duane. You're single and raising two kids!"

"Gimme a break, Sarge. I'm fine, I'm fine!"

I look at Duane. A part of me knows better. But he's a good officer, trustworthy and his cheerful face is hard to resist. I hesitate, then relent. "OK, you can work, Duane. Just be careful, will ya?" He grins. "Thanks, Sarge!" I ignore a tinge of remorse. He'll be fine. Always is.

It's after midnight and I'm on the freeway when dispatch calls and asks me to go to a private radio channel. "We have a CHP officer in a possible 11-44 (fatal accident) at 80 and Interstate 5."

> I'm there within five minutes and a patrolman points to a yellow blanket alongside the road. A short distance beyond I spot Duane's private motorcycle on its side. Apparently, on his way home after working the overtime, he had fallen asleep, wandered off the road and struck a signpost with his head.
>
> I kneel down and pull back the blanket in the dark. Half of Duane's head is gone, and the groan comes deep from my gut. I stare at the wreckage of his head several minutes, holding the blanket and finally I realize I'm repeating, over and over, "Oh, Duane . . . oh, Duane . . ."
>
> I blame myself for letting him work. I remember that part of me that had wanted to send him home. He'd be safe, asleep, with his kids. I'm not able to forget this one.
>
> I continued to blame myself for allowing Duane to work and for his death. I held this belief for years, in spite of the fact that Duane had stopped off at a favorite drinking spot and was intoxicated at the time of his death. I had to have been aware of this at the time of the investigation, but I blocked it from my mind. A fellow retiree reminded me of this fact years later and I was completely surprised.

I still held it together for a time but things were unraveling faster, catching up with me. Memories, the demons, the dirty secrets, the faces, the ghosts were all being stirred up. They were turning into nightmares, daydreams, anxiety attacks, flashes of anger and rage, and unpredictability. On one afternoon, uncharacteristic of me, I began shouting at a complainant on the telephone. By the time I slammed the phone down, the entire office was silent. In a fog, I recall a secretary sitting and asking, repeatedly, "Are you all right? Are you all right? Are you all right. . . ?"

> I'm enjoying lunch at a restaurant down the street from highway patrol headquarters with two coworkers. Two of us were are in full uniform and are pleasantly engaged in conversation when a high-ranking highway patrol commander in civilian clothes with whom I am only slightly familiar tiptoes up behind me from another table and, taking a handful of saltine crackers, showers them all over my head and uniform. I'm covered, head and shoulders. He then prances, cackling, back to his fellow command staffers.
>
> For those unfamiliar with police culture, at least for veterans, to do something like this to a fellow officer in a public restaurant is a disgrace and insult, not just to the individual, but to the uniform he is wearing. I freeze in shock, as does everyone in the restaurant, which falls silent. A waitress with a tray stops, frozen and staring. The only

sound is the giggling of the commander and his companions. Finally, catching my composure, I brush the crackers off my uniform, gather what dignity remains, and attempt to resume our lunch and conversation.

This event did not come up again until years later in an interview with a psychiatrist. He sat for a moment, shocked, and asked, "Why would he do something like that?" My answer, voice trembling with anger, was, "You'd have to dig into his sick little mind to figure that out." The psychiatrist asked nothing more.

Departmental betrayal takes many forms and is pointed out by many officers as one of the highest stressors in police work. This is a slightly misunderstood concept, of course, a bit too loosely tossed around. With exceptions, it would be a rarity that an officer would fall prey to PTSD or commit suicide exclusively because of trauma experienced within the office or from an administrative action alone. More likely, one could expect a case of PTSD to occur as the result of administrative interference or misinterpretation and lack of understanding of a field event. It is *this* kind of frustration that officers react to with great anger, feeling a tremendous sense of betrayal and lack of trust. As one veteran officer explained to me, "The dangers aren't out on the road. The dangers are in the office when you drive back in." There, he explained, the language is alien and the world is seen through entirely different glasses. Reality "goes out the window." He added, "You just sign whatever paper they give you, wipe your rear with it, and go do your job again."

As the manifestations of PTSD increase, the impacts on the family system grow and it becomes a vicious circle, dragging everyone down with it. Depression, a common companion of PTSD, is frightening, as are the anxiety attacks, the inability to sleep, the flashbacks, and the rages experienced by the victim.

Terrible evening, I wrote in my journal. Agitated, "crawly." Can't relax, even since my [anxiety] pill. I hate this. Damn them all. I keep pacing, then sit and make notes. Why? Anxious and scared. I find a chair in a spare room and put some relaxing music on. The foot is tapping. I know it and I hate it and can't stop it.

My daughter (ten) comes upstairs and looks in and quietly suggests, "Dad, there's a good movie just starting – "

"Shut the HELL up!"

In an instant, she has disappeared from the door. I immediately feel regret and follow her. She's sitting on the floor, back to me and

watching the television. My wife looks over at me and asks, "What was that all about?"
I ignore her and say to my daughter, "Terry, I am so sorry I shouted at you like that." She didn't move. "I really am sorry – I don't know what's wrong with me." She nodded slightly, her back still to me. I look at my wife, who just shakes her head in a motion to "drop it." I go back upstairs and the darkness grows deeper.

Above all others was that farm worker trying to take my gun. This was the one face I could never escape, and the scenario kept haunting me more than any other, well into my therapy. Leading up to my suicide attempt, his face would appear and I could hear his voice, laughing and calling me "coward," over and over. I dreamed of him in countless scenarios. One I wrote down immediately after waking in a sweat:

It is dark, I wrote. I drive to the office and, at each freeway off-ramp, I see small groups of officers huddled, waiting. All are in full dress gear, with parade jackets and gold aiguillettes and shining brass. They stare at me as I pass. The office gates are locked and the windows dark. I go to the front door, where I find my uniforms stacked neatly outside. I peer into the glass door and am met by my own reflection. I tap and the door opens automatically and I go inside. It's deathly silent and I go past the counter and followed the hallway to the briefing room, where I can hear voices.
When I enter, the room is brilliantly lit and crowded with officers in parade gear. They all fall silent and stare at me. There is one chair at the front facing the room and I know it's for me. I sit.
"You're late," one officer says.
"Yes," says another, "we've been here for hours."
"But why?" I plead.
"You asked us here," one points out, "to explain why you won't come back."
"Cowardice is a perfectly valid reason," says a senior officer matter-of-factly.
"But I'm not a coward. I'm not. I'm not!"
"We know you're a coward because you failed the tests."
"What tests?" I ask, surprised.
"You know them – you've been taking them all along. You just thought we weren't keeping track of your scores."
"You mean – "
"We saw everything? Yes. We saw everything."
"You must have seen all the good things I did!"

"Those don't count. Not when you're a coward."
"But I'm not really a coward. I've just been scared, sometimes. Sometimes I didn't know what to do."
"Same thing!" several laugh. "Same thing."
"No."
"Yes!"
"You could come back."
"You would let me come back?"
"Of course. Under one condition."
"What condition?"
"That you not be cowardly."
"Can I promise that?"
"The doctor knows." All eyes turn to the back of the room, where a balding man in a three-piece suit stands up. "I am a psychiatrist," he tells me.
"Yes," I answer, encouraged. "Then you understand what is happening to me, don't you?"
"I do," smiles the doctor. "In fact, I've made a diagnosis."
"What is your diagnosis?"
"You are a coward!"
The room erupts in wild laughter as I jump up from my chair, crying wildly.
"No," I scream. "It can't be over like that, please – "

My entry is May 30:

Missed my therapy appointment today. Don't care. The clock means nothing. I'm like a ghost around the house. Hear people laughing when I'm hiding upstairs. Stops when I go down. No small wonder, I look like the grim reaper. Same grey bathrobe all the time. Try not to look in mirror. Huge black cloud in and around me. Feeling I've failed everyone, everyone around me scared of me, me scared of me. Day and night don't matter. Sometimes I sleep, wake up, sleep. The faces and the nightmares come and now I just feel lost with them. I beg them to leave me alone but they keep on coming. They don't care. Like vultures picking on a dead body. Please help me, God. I'm so scared. Bring me to you if that's where I belong. Is that where peace is?

May 31.

I decide to go out today, get myself a haircut. Way overdue. Shower and shave off several days of beard. Cheeks are hollow. I look like someone who has been in solitary confinement for a month. The sun

is shining. Lisa is happy to see me going outside. I try to smile as I put on clean clothes and grab the car keys. She's hoping I feel better, that it's a good sign. Maybe the meds are working. I feel dark and empty. Maybe the sun will change that.
The barber chair feels good. Hair all over while he jabbers and sprays the good smelling stuff from a bottle on my hair. Neck feels good and I swing through the door into the sun and head home.

I'm taking the same route I've driven for years, I write, when suddenly nothing makes sense. I recognize a little concrete bridge but it's in the wrong place. I'm going the wrong way, I realize. I turn around and now I don't recognize the street at all. I turn around again and someone honks at me. The street signs have strange names. I pull to the side of the street and look around. Nothing is familiar. It dawns on me – I'm lost. I begin to cry, first in chokes and, then, sobbing uncontrollably. I'm *lost.* I've never been lost since I was little. Someone is walking by. They pause and look at me, then hurry on. I'm angry but the tears are still running.

When I dry up I stop and catch my breath. The sun is still out but it seems terribly dark and frightening to me. I'm exhausted and I have to go home. I pull out and the little bridge is suddenly in the right place. Just beyond it is the street where I turn. In moments I'm home.

Lisa compliments my haircut. I try to hold back, but I break into tears again, telling her how scared I was to have gotten lost in an area I had been driving for so many years. She tries to be reassuring, but she's frightened as well. I gather my composure and head up the stairs. Into the dark room, where I belong. With the faces and my failure. I failed again. I sit and look out the window at the sunlight while the old faces come and go and a woman screams. I've given up trying to keep them away.

June 3. Was determined to sleep and hide from everything last night. Took two sleeping pills. No dreams, no dreams. Slept 12 to 13 hours. Very ashamed of myself today. Lisa at work, kids in school. Took my gun and sat on the floor in the bedroom for a while. Thought about it and put it back in the closet. Almost went next door, maybe talk to neighbor. Why? I'd say something and scare them. I'm already killing my wife piece by piece. They're walking on eggs, scared of my every move, scared I'll scream at them, scared of what I look like.
Called my therapist just to talk. She called back and I told her I was doing about the same. Felt good to know she was there for a minute. I need to listen to what she's saying. I know I'm fighting and I don't

know why. I HATE all of this and everyone must think I'm *choosing* to do it to myself but why can't I see it that way?
I need to forget yesterday ever happened.
The hurt is so deep. Sad. Lonely. Furious.
Was I born to hurt like this? What are these awful things that have come into me and killed me? ISN'T THERE ANYTHING LEFT?
Can't write any more.

I close the journal, set it high on a shelf in the closet, and pull out my six-inch revolver again. I've carried it for twenty-three years. Originally, at the academy, it had belonged to one of the four officers murdered in the 1970 shootout in Newhall, California. He had problems with it. After repairs, it had been reissued to me. I don't know if that means anything. I feel slightly sick to my stomach.

I sit down on the floor in the bedroom, leaning up against the bed. There is a loud, rushing sound in my ears and my heart is skipping fast. My breathing is excited and the air against my nose and mouth is cold. I sit up straight, gun in my lap, and fight to catch my breath. I feel a little dizzy. Kind of like it felt after the man in the ditch. Maybe that's how it's supposed to be. I make myself calm down and my breathing returns to normal. I turn the gun in my hand, pop open the cylinder and spill the bullets into my empty hand. I reload it, one bullet at a time, and return the gun to my lap.

I try to remember how I got here and I can't. I'm just so tired. I'm slipping under the water, and I've been fighting to stay afloat so long that I'm just so tired and I want to just sink down and let the water take me, fill my lungs and let me rest without any more fighting. All around me are enemies – the faces, the screamers, the angry and the hurt and the sad, the CHP, and everyone who knows how weak I am. I've failed at so many things.

I let myself down
my kids
I let my kids down
tortured them
a drunk, a coward
and my wife too – so many smiles I took away
Oh, Duane . . .
selfish
mean
so much pain, like a knife
monsters, sick people, screaming and hating

> I'm so sorry, God. Do you really forgive? You can't forgive me, can you? I let you down, everyone, and it hurts
> Oh God it hurts so very deep so so very deep and even curling up doesn't help make the hurt go away

I straighten up against the bed and raise the gun to my head. Quick, which way? Under the chin. Oh, God, horrible all over. Side of the head. I grab the barrel with my other hand to steady it against my skull. The wall begins to vibrate and there is a rumbling sound. Vibration and rumbling. The wall shaking? What?

I lower the gun and listen. I understand. It's the electric garage door opening on the other side of the bedroom wall. My wife and daughter are home. Startled into reality, I look at the gun in my hand and drop it like it was scalding hot. What have I done, what am I doing – *what do I do now?* I jump to my feet and almost fall as the blood rushes from my head. I retrieve the gun from the floor and shove it up on the closet shelf and turn around just as my wife walks into the bedroom. Lisa sees my face, flushed with panic. She looks at me, then at the open closet behind me. "What's going on?" she asks with alarm.

She sits on the edge of the bed and waits for an answer. I stand awkwardly and glance over at myself in the mirror. I don't recognize the face. "I'm in trouble," I admit, turning to face her. I take a deep breath and release it slowly. "I was going to kill myself." She nodded and looked over at the closet. She knew where I kept my revolver. "The gun?"

"Yes."

"I'm not going to tell you, Andy. You know what to do."

"Yes I do."

"You make the call and I'll take care of the gun." I nod.

I hear the front door close as I dial the doctor's office and leave an emergency message. Lisa is taking the gun to a neighbor's for safekeeping. It's the only one we own. Within an hour, I've packed a small bag and I'm on the freeway to a psychiatric hospital. I insisted on driving myself – a token effort at control that took away some of the helplessness.

I'm surprised by the hospital. After being admitted and shown to my room, I'm turned over to Tom, another patient, to be shown around the facility. Tom isn't drooling or babbling, nor is anyone else. They all seem genuinely pleased to see me. Tom introduces himself as a computer programmer. I tell him I'm a cop and he seems only mildly interested. I'm a patient, here. There are no cells. I do notice the windows are breakproof and there are nicks and deep scratches on some.

There are rules I have to get used to, such as needing permission to go outside. The cafeteria is off limits except at meal times, but Tom promises he'll show me how to sneak several ice creams out after meals.

The furniture is designed for lots of sitting and group therapy, I learn. Hours of it. Over the next three weeks, I'll get to know patients intimately – and they'll know me. I'm also a lab rat. These are the weeks that they really focus on medications and finding the right combination for me – I'm a captive audience, and what better way to monitor me? My own doctor comes, daily, and I have individual therapy sessions in addition to the group therapy. It's a "talking place." None of us arrive wanting to talk, but by the time we leave, we're talkers. It's the beginning of a long journey to recovery.

Strangely, we also learn a special kind of laughter that only depressed people can share with one another. It comes from the special bond formed by knowing, intimately, the journey they're on. No one else can laugh in the dark like they can. I do engage in one rebellion. I have a fellow mutineer who, like me, is willing to risk a padded cell on principal. Art therapy begins the second week. Valerie is an elementary school teacher and has been "teaching art to bratty little kids" her entire life. As a cop, I'm not going to cut paper dolls or finger paint. Art therapy begins the second week. We refuse to attend.

Our insurrection lasts one day, to the delight of the other patients. Then we learn that we are there to participate – or we aren't there any longer. We cave. The room is intense with patients cutting pictures out of magazines, sketching pictures, pasting things, or wiring mobiles together. Valerie and I are both studiously selecting variously colored beads and sliding them onto thin wires that are deliberately too short for strangulation.

Suddenly, Valerie slaps her beads down on the table and cries out, "It's finally come to this! A lifetime of working and here we are – stringing beads in a mental institution!" The room explodes into laughter. I lean back in my chair, enjoying the first glimpse of joy I've felt in years.

EPILOGUE

The medications are working well. I continue in therapy and I'm doing an early morning paper route to keep busy. My retirement papers are in process. The process of healing is a long one – I'm told it can take years. Healing things with my family may take longer. They, too, have been through trauma. The law enforcement career, PTSD, and mental illness in general can have a devastating impact on everyone involved, and it has nearly destroyed the relationship I once had with my wife and children.

Shortly before he passed away, I had dinner with an old friend who had worked for me when I was a sergeant. I was fond of Sam because he thought sergeants were worthless and was always quick to remind me of that. After I retired, he told me I was the best sergeant he had ever worked for. I wasn't sure if that still meant I was worthless, and I was afraid to ask.

After dinner, we sat out in the car for a while listening to the rain pound on the roof, and I felt safe telling him my secret of the man in the ditch. Sam listened without a word, then just put his head back, closed his eyes and sighed. "Sarge," he finally said. "You're only a coward if you call yourself that, and it sounds like that's what you've been doing for too many years. You did the only thing any cop could do to survive. But you also kept on going. You could have drunk yourself to death and you could have taken a shortcut and blown your brains out. But you didn't. You're still going. Do something with it." Sam thrust out a beefy hand. *You did good, even for a sergeant.*

It's early afternoon on a hot summer afternoon and I sit on the front step with the mail. The first envelope I come to has a return address from the Department of California Highway Patrol. My heart misses a beat or two and I open it.

> Dear Sergeant O'Hara, it begins.
> The Department must be concerned when an employee is diagnosed as having a psychological or emotional disability which may result in the employee acting inappropriately or violently.
> When such a condition is present, the Department may find it necessary to suspend peace officer powers and to obtain State-issued weapons that are in the employee's possession.
> Medical information was received which indicates that you have a psychological disorder and that you have periods of extreme anger,

> rage, anxiety and fears about getting out of control and acting on your impulses.
> We understand that you have already turned in your State-issued weapon. In the event you have additional State property, please turn that in as well. Although this may be a disappointment to you, I hope you can appreciate the necessity of our decision and trust you will refrain from carrying a concealed or loaded firearm.
> We hope you will be feeling better soon, and extend our best wishes for the future. We sincerely appreciate the years of service you have provided the Department.
>
> It's signed by the Commissioner.

I let the paper dangle between my thumb and forefinger and the warm breeze catches and flaps it around. The sun feels good today. The guy across the street is mowing his lawn. I'm going to do the same thing. I have a lot of work to do.

REFERENCES

Anderson, B., & Dahlgren, E. (2002, June 26). When job stress becomes disabling. *Business Week Magazine.*

Chapter 6

LOOKING FOR NEW PREVENTION ALTERNATIVES: THE BADGE OF LIFE EMOTIONAL SELF-CARE TRAINING

ANDREW F. O'HARA

Insanity: doing the same thing over and over again and expecting different results.

Albert Einstein

INTRODUCTION

Today's police suicide prevention programs face major challenges (Violanti, 2007). The forces of change in American society in the twenty-first century are placing new and great stresses on law enforcement to adapt, shift, and innovate in ways never before imagined. Economic forces, generational shifts, and unforeseen cultural conflicts are putting pressure on traditional police roles and responsibilities. All this creates additional pressure on an occupation already known for its caustic work environment. If we are to support our law enforcement personnel in what they do, we must closely reevaluate what we are doing, not only to prevent suicides but also to provide the tools they need to survive emotionally.

The task we face is no longer just about suicide. It is time to start looking at the stresses and pressures *all* our officers are facing and provide them with the resources they need for healthy emotional self-care. This requires a major shift in our current programs. We need to examine how we set our goals, how we determine our strategies, and the manner in which we use our resources.

Our programs sometimes seem full of contradictions and anomalies. One might ask, for example, why we even *have* police suicide prevention programs when no police suicide has ever been the result of work-related PTSD. It certainly seems like an act of great benevolence, on the part of police departments, to invest so much time and money into something that has nothing at all to do with law enforcement.

The question may seem like a bit of amusing hyperbole, but it becomes quite deadly when it is pointed out that, by refusing to acknowledge the work-relatedness of any police suicides at all, police departments are hiding information that could save future police officer lives.

So let us look at what truth we can find, recognizing that some police suicides are, by reading between the obvious lines, the result of line of duty emotional trauma.

- The number one killer of police officers is accidents.
- The number two killer of police officers is suicide.
- The number three killer of police officers is homicide.

Nationally, 2008 saw 141 suicides out of 883,600 officers in the United States. This resulted in a suicide rate of 16/100,000 compared to the public rate of 11/100,000 and the Army's rate of 20/100,000 during war. On average, police officers take their own lives every 2.58 days, or every sixty hours.

No one can argue that police suicides are a tragedy. That is not the issue. However, we are going to look at the numbers from several very new perspectives. We will do this by putting them under a harsh lamp that is intended to help us highlight what is best for our officers, not necessarily what is comfortable.

If nothing changes, nothing changes. The stagnation of our programs is our enemy, especially when the number of police suicides continues to increase and what we are doing is not making a difference. When this happens, we must look at those strategies. If we do not, we continue aimlessly on, making lame excuses such as "If it hadn't been for us, the numbers would have been even higher" or, worse, "There was nothing more we could do."

In this chapter, we are introducing a new program called the Emotional Self-Care (ESC) training program. It is designed to work, in concert, with existing suicide prevention programs. The former is *proactive*, the latter is *reactive.* We must have both, and they have to work together if we truly want to save lives, physically and emotionally, in our ranks. The term reactive is not intended as a negative; for purposes of this discussion, it is used merely to differentiate the roles of suicide prevention and our new proposed program in relation to suicide. The concept is simple. It is no longer "just" about suicide. It is about mental health for *all* police officers.

THE NUMBERS

Although police suicide numbers and the rates are alarming, an analytical side of the picture must be examined if we hope to get anywhere. The fact is that 141 suicides out of a total force of 883,600 are statistically microscopic. Startling, but true. This raw number, 141, represents 0.0001595 percent of the law enforcement workforce. This is not unusual. No matter what population one examines, suicide is found to be at such a low rate of behavior.

With what magic butterfly net do we expect we can race back and forth across the United States and catch 141 suicides among more than three quarters of a million police officers? This is what we have been trying to do for years. Making it worse is the fact that more than three quarters of the police suicides "slipped through the cracks" unnoticed. No one saw them coming. We do not know the number of suicide attempts. Our 141 grains of sand keep getting harder to spot, especially when they look just like the other three quarters of a million. It is time to start looking at some new approaches to an old problem.

Living, breathing officers are experiencing medically verified cases of work-related PTSD and becoming *suicidal* (but stopping short of suicide). Others are silent, not letting anyone know what is going on inside. For example, a study by Robinson, Sigman, and Wilson (1997) of suburban police officers found 13 percent met the criteria for PTSD. General anxiety disorders run at 3.1 percent and depression at 6.7 percent for the public. Given the fact that the suicide rate for police officers is already higher than that for the general population, one can surmise that the rate of depression, particularly among veteran officers, is also higher. The significant exposure to trauma may ultimately have a negative impact on the emergency responder's processes of cognition and perception (McCann & Pearlman, 1990).

Although the general population may recognize the existence of horrific trauma, they do not experience it as law enforcement officers do. In performing their duties, officers cannot protect themselves from acknowledging the reality that such trauma does exist. This then raises, for the officer, the added specter (and stressor) of potential trauma in their own lives. (Atkinson-Taylor, 2003).

At only 5 to 10 percent, we are left with as many as 70,500 to 141,000 police officers who could use help with their emotional well-being. Thus, one out of every twelve officers (or worse, one out of every six) could benefit from therapy or some other level of mental health assistance. The chances of reaching 141 officers (every 6262th officer) with the traditional suicide prevention program are dismally low. The odds of reaching 70,500 to 140,000 out of 883,600 officers with an emotional self-care program designed to keep officers healthy are much higher. We are now looking at more than a few grains of sand among almost a million others that are all moving.

WHY POLICE OFFICERS COMMIT SUICIDE

No one has *a clear idea* why police officers commit suicide. Police chiefs refuse to discuss it. To our knowledge, not a single police suicide in the United States in the last twenty years has been attributed to a line-of-duty cause (PTSD or other trauma-related reason). Officers can, we know, get PTSD on the job. They can become suicidal because of the job, but it is impossible for them to commit suicide because of the job. (The Public Safety Officers' Benefits Program provides a definition solely for the purpose of giving benefits and has nothing to do with whether or not an officer's suicide was caused by work-related trauma – it was or it was not.)

Still, we *can* make several safe assumptions:

- The .0001595 percent of officers who committed suicide in 2008 were not the *only* ones experiencing emotional problems.
- During 2008, 70,500 to 141,000 officers continued to work while suffering silently from undiagnosed PTSD, other anxiety disorders, or other manifestations of the stress and trauma they have experienced in their careers.
- Living, breathing officers are submitting disability claims for PTSD and having them medically approved.

- It is common sense to assume that at least *one* police suicide per year is the result of PTSD suffered in the line of duty (Bonokoski, 2009; Nocera, 2009).

TRADITIONAL SUICIDE PREVENTION PROGRAMS

For years, police psychologists and departments have relied on a relatively standard "suicide prevention" model to deal with a seeming tidal wave of police suicides. This widespread alarm was fed by inflated estimates of police suicide numbers that had no basis in fact but were spread by lecturers and then the news media. It was accepted that officers were falling faster than once a day, for a total of 400 or more a year, at rates of approximately 50/100,000 (more than double the U.S. Army during a time of war). A near-siege mentality set in. Departments rushed to hire staff psychologists. Employee assistance units were set up and staffed. Peer support officers were selected. Power points, posters and videos were thrown together and hastily trained instructors made the rounds of squads, selling the importance of officers watching one another for signs of suicide and urging them to ask for help if they found themselves in trouble. Numerous suicide prevention organizations appeared on the internet, offering programs of varying content and quality and many sharing some common themes.

- *Caretaker elements*, in which officers were to be instructed to memorize suicide warning signs and monitor one another for them.
- *Get help when you need it* messages.
- Posters with tormented officers holding guns or hands reaching for guns and headlines such as *Grab a Phone, Not Your Gun.*
- *Contract counseling services* (employee assistance) for varying numbers of free therapy visits.

With the exception of peer support, one limitation of these programs was that they were *externally* focused – urging minimal attention by the individual over his or her own emotional well-being. The drive has been on the observation of others, and watching for the symptoms. The only time that self-appraisal or diagnosis has been important is when the officer is "in trouble," at which time he or she is encouraged to seek help.

To illustrate the dilemma we face with the typical suicide prevention program, we use the Humpty Dumpty rhyme. The king's soldiers place a row of police officers (Humpty Dumptys) on the wall and then sit below, waiting in case one falls. From time to time, they encourage them not to fall. "Don't fall, Humpty Dumptys" they cry. "Let someone know if you think you're about to fall."

Satisfied that everyone has heard their message and that all is well, the king's soldiers nestle down for the night in their positions. All of a sudden, one of the Humpty Dumptys takes a great fall and breaks. The soldiers look at one another in shock and ask, "Did you know a Humpty Dumpty was about to fall?" With great consternation, they shout up to the Humpty Dumptys on the wall. "Did any of you see any signs that your comrade was about to fall?" Greatly distressed, the Humpty Dumptys respond. "It was a surprise!" Several cry out, "He seemed normal enough to us!" All insist they had seen nothing out of the ordinary.

In the morning, the soldiers tell the king the bad news. "It was not our fault," they insist. "It was a shock. We told all the Humpty Dumptys to be careful and to let us know if they were in trouble." The King nods and is satisfied that everything had been done to keep the Humpty Dumptys from harm. They find another Humpty Dumpty to fill the empty space on the wall.

We draw this comparison to make an important point. The king, his soldiers, and all the Humpty Dumptys were doing the best they could do. Unfortunately, they were missing a big piece of the information: self-preparation. No one was training the Humpty Dumptys on how to sit safely on the wall and not fall off. There were all kinds of alternatives – steadying themselves with their hands, losing weight so as to not topple, even wearing seatbelts. Some, such as the latter, should have come from the king, but no one bothered to think. They sent the Humpty Dumptys up into danger, gave them warnings, and were surprised when they fell.

Caretaker programs have been around many years. The greatest drawback is not in the programs themselves. The problem is that they are "end stage," when an officer is in trouble or in danger of suicide. This should not change. This is actually what a suicide prevention program should be. What must change, however, is training and programs that do more than try to snatch our personnel back from the cliff or stop them from falling off the wall. We need to remember that we need more than suicide prevention. We need a healthy police force.

A NEW APPROACH: THE ESC TRAINING PROGRAM

The ESC training program is based on two simple principles: (1) each officer will be responsible for his or her *own* emotional well-being, and (2) a department is responsible for providing the career-long training, tools, and resources with which an officer can meet that responsibility.

The guiding principal of ESC training is that every police officer is a potential trauma victim – every workday. As Anderson and Dahlgren wrote, "In some ways, a cop's work may be even more traumatic than that of a soldier sent into a war zone. The police officer's job, over many years, exposes and re-exposes them to traumatic events that would make anybody recoil in horror." (Anderson & Dahlgren, 2002).

With this in mind, the goal of ESC training is a form of aggressive prevention that involves *every officer* – not just officers who are suicidal and not just officers who are "in trouble." ESC is a fitness program. In the same way that running and swimming are forms of physical fitness, ESC is a form of mental fitness. It provides officers with the training and resources by which they can avoid *getting* into trouble or *becoming* suicidal. It does this through two key elements:

- Annual training
  - Types and signs of trauma
  - Recognition of traumatization and measures to take, immediate and long term
  - Stress management
  - Resilience
  - Healthy lifestyles
  - The importance of suicide prevention (which is taught separately)
- Annual Mental Health Checks: voluntary, confidential, without reporting or accountability to the department

ESC is designed to begin with the *healthy* officer but will as a matter of course include officers who are having difficulties. Suicide prevention is presented as a separate class. ESC should start at the academy and continue annually until retirement. Although it can begin at any stage of an officer's career, it should become a "cradle to the grave" process in a department. Mental health, particularly in the caustic, brutal world of law enforcement, is not something we focus on the first year and is forgotten for the next twenty-nine.

Peer support officers are the key players in making ESC happen. They provide the ESC training, both at the academy and in the field, encourage officers to use ESC resources, and form the link to the ESC partner program, suicide prevention. Trauma can be expected to happen in spite of ESC. Regardless of an officer's best efforts to maintain a healthy lifestyle, physically and emotionally, events and circumstances can be overwhelming; PTSD, depression, and other disorders can set in; suicidal tendencies can develop; and the need for clinical intervention becomes necessary. Further, not all officers can be expected to follow their training and pursue good emotional self-care any more than they do healthy physical health training. This is where the suicide prevention program will always be needed and would come into play.

ESC, however, is preparation and proactive prevention in its truest sense. It is based on the premise that, if we are to ultimately influence police suicides in the end, we must address the reasons that could put a gun in an officer's hand to begin with. With the implementation of ESC, we are actually completing an equation, a formula. Suicide prevention programs are one half of the formula. They provide intervention and care at one end of the spectrum – for officers in trouble and officers who may be in danger of taking their own lives.

Our training and resources must acknowledge that the police environment is one of the most caustic imaginable. Officers are affected by it over ten, twenty, and thirty years. The pressures often continue in spite of promotion, as shown by a high number of sergeants, lieutenants, captains, and chiefs who committed suicide in 2008 to 2009. Many, as the years and decades go by, become the "walking wounded." They do not commit suicide, nor do they open themselves up to therapy or other help. They "man up," survive, and enter retirement as unhappy, tortured individuals doomed to a shortened life.

ESC'S ANNUAL MENTAL HEALTH CHECKS

The annual mental health check is the most important part of ESC. It is a total shift from the traditional focus used in past years. Therapy has been something to turn to only when the officer "needs help." Now we say, "See a therapist whether you need help or not." ESC programs must be more than waiting until a "crisis" or a potential suicide arrives. They must be long-term – *true* prevention. Visits must be confidential and the department must do no tracking. It must require no reporting on whether an officer goes or not. If an officer does not "trust" anything connected with the department, we encourage him or her to seek out a private counselor and pay the co-pay.

How the Annual Mental Health Check Works

The key to the annual mental health check is that it is for all officers, not merely those experiencing problems. For those who would say they do not "need" a therapist, the point must be made that this is *preventative.* If they still reject it, this is fine. They may still participate, unknown to us – now, a month later, several years later, or never.

It is also vital that officers understand that mental health checks are *choices.* Whether they are officers, deputies, sergeants, captains, or chiefs, no one can force them to make healthy choices. No one, for example, can force them to brush their teeth. Absurd as it sounds, they are free to let them rot. No one can force them to follow a good diet. No one will ever force them to get an annual physical exam, a flu shot, inoculate their children, or change the oil in their cars. Similarly, no one can force them to take care of their physical or mental health.

The following are some goals or opportunities for a series of officer sessions, all worthy of mention during annual training.

1. Look at the past year. This includes one's personal and professional lives. Although many police suicides are attributed to family problems, there is a possibility that the problems at home resulted from work stress and trauma. The past year provides the information base from which one can learn and grow. These are the preparation for future trauma that an officer needs – similar to an annual inoculation. The individual picks out situations that were emotionally challenging and evaluates their response. It may take some repeated probing and some self-discovery to work through it. Previously undisclosed traumatic work experiences may be identified, discussed, and treated, rather than allowing them to worsen.

2. Apply the past year's experience to the next – set *goals.* This goes beyond a performance evaluation or a New Year's resolution. It involves the discovery of what tools will work best in stressful or trau-

matic situations – or in the marriage. Stress management techniques, such as diet, exercise and breathing, can be customized to the individual and trigger points identified for their use. The recognition of traumatization and what actions officers should take if they feel themselves becoming overwhelmed during or after an event are important.

3. Identify and address problem areas. Officers may have specific difficulties they want to talk about, such as marital issues, substance abuse, financial fears, interpersonal issues with peers or supervisors, or fears and insecurities they feel uncomfortable discussing elsewhere.

4. Learn and develop strengths (resiliencies). The greatest step in the development of resilience is when individuals pass beyond what everyone else tells them it is and determine what it is for themselves. Developing strengths also includes identifying techniques for internal management of stress and traumatic situations when encountered, healthy emotional disengagement, recognition of inner alarm signals and aftercare for the self, strategies for dealing with signs of trauma and triggers, and other healthy emotional self-care techniques.

5. Develop a working and trust relationship with a therapist in case it is needed. Because career law enforcement officers are committing themselves to as many as two or three decades in uniform, it is highly advantageous that they have a clinician they can turn to with issues on an ongoing basis.

ACADEMY ESC TRAINING

A law enforcement officer's commitment upon entering the academy is not a light one. Because good mental health is as important to street survival as prowess with a gun is, it is essential that training begin in the academy and continue after he or she leaves.

In the past two decades, academy emphasis has been on a "pseudo–boot camp" model, motivated by a belief that there must be compensation for the shortage of military veterans among recruits. Unfortunately, sending new officers out with a belief that they are invincible and superhuman is short lived in the field. How much more important it is that we send them out understanding not *what* the traumas are but *how* to handle stress and trauma, as well as maintain and continue to grow in their emotional health as peace officers.

The subject matter necessary to prepare cadets properly for stress and trauma should parallel that given to veteran officers. There should be no change in subject matter, only the depth to which it is explored. For departments willing to invest in the health of their new personnel, it would be ideal for a peer support officer from outside the academy to team with a therapist in presenting the material in weekly segments. Upon completion of the training blocks, any additional time an academy is willing to provide could be used to great benefit in "modeling" therapy in the classroom with the cadets as a class.

Sadly, we start officers in academies by teaching them the art of disguise, of facade. They walk the same, look the same, square corners the same, sit and stand the same way, and shout "ew-RAH" at the slightest cue. They are nameless and faceless. The facade they learn goes far to explain why three quarters of police suicides are a total "surprise" each year. Amazingly, we are teaching officers to watch other officers for suicidal signs when the very ones they are watching are masters of disguise – and we taught them to be that way!

In this kind of spartan atmosphere, exchanges of emotion are discouraged, and cadets graduate with what researchers have called an "adolescent sense of invincibility." The mindset upon leaving many academies is to be a "warrior" and show no weakness (emotion). This need to maintain a facade over feelings is reinforced by the existing culture throughout an officer's career. Academy instructors push cadets to exercise 200 to 300 hours per year when they leave the academy. In contrast, few are encouraged to invest a single hour or two during the year in their mental health or in seeing a therapist.

Academies require 40 to 60 hours of firearms training. Some offer as many as 100 hours of emergency vehicle operations training (EVOC). Rare is the academy, however, that offers more than a token two or three hours of Power Point presentations on suicide prevention or mental health.

This is the first part of an officer's training that has to change – the limited amount of time expended on mental health at our police academies, even if it must be taken from other programs. Few would suggest later that a depressed, alcoholic officer is going to perform well in a high-speed pursuit. Who believes that an officer wracked with guilt for a mistake that cost a life the night before is going to be alert while searching for a suspect in a dark neighborhood?

FIELD TRAINING

After academy training, all officers should have *annual* training with a peer support officer and, if possible, a therapist familiar with law enforcement that includes

- The difference between stress and trauma. There are clear differences between *stress* and *trauma*. These words are frequently confused and used interchangeably.
- Stress happens. Negative stress happens as a condition of today's modern life, particularly law enforcement. Stress, however, can managed by exercise; diet; good rest; time management; healthy sex; quality time with family; maintaining rounded outside relationships and hobbies or sports; moderation in habits such as alcohol, therapy, and more.
- Trauma happens *to* you. PTSD is the one psychological disorder known to have a purely external cause, thus we refer to it as an injury.
- Trauma comes in two forms: critical and cumulative. The critical incident is generally easy to spot – the shootout, the death of an officer or partner, the loss of an infant. Cumulative trauma, on the other hand, is far more difficult to identify, even for the victim officer, and may be of a long-delayed onset.
  - *Critical trauma* is well-understood in law enforcement as the "headline" event – the shootings, the loss of a partner, the infant deaths, the terribly gruesome accidents, witnessing a suicide, being involved in an accident, and other singularly dramatic events.
  - *Cumulative trauma*, however, is rarely recognized or acted on until it begins to have a negative effect on the officer. Often, a minor incident can trigger a reaction, or it may be a critical incident that combines with a series of others over a period of time, even years, to trigger an onset of PTSD.
- The myths behind mental illness and suicide. This is an opportunity to address stigma and the nature of suicide, explaining that suicide is the result of a mental disorder, not a choice. Officers continue to call police suicides "cowardly" and "selfish." Training must debunk myths and discourage insensitive comments such as
  - *Suicide is a selfish, angry act.*
  - *Suicide is a cowardly act.*

– *Suicide is a permanent solution to a temporary problem.*

- The value and development of resilience. It is helpful that officers understand resiliency as one of their tools in their ESC toolbox. Finding an awareness of one's own strengths and then expanding it with each year is not a classroom exercise; it is an individual one, best accomplished with a therapist's assistance. Although they may or may not be addressed specifically, understanding the concepts can give the officer a feeling of purpose as a visit approaches. One's ability to nurture it gives a crucial element of control and hope in a world that officers find threatening and confusing. Resiliency is as valuable as one's ability to pump iron and prowess on the range.

All cadets, all police officers have a certain amount of resiliency or they would not have made it as far as they have. Resilience is, simply put, the ability to bounce back. It is an individual learning process and not a classroom exercise. The development of this set of strengths is one of the keys to preparing officers for the challenges ahead – the stressors and the traumas.

- The value of mental health checks
- Stress management
- Trauma recognition and management of trauma both immediate and long term
- Emotional scene management techniques ("empathetic disengagement")

THE BIG QUESTION – WHY SO MUCH FOCUS ON "HEALTHY OFFICERS?"

Here we stand, telling a bunch of hardened cops, "See a therapist every year, whether you need to or not."

They won't buy this! you say.

Some will not. Many of these are already cynical and bitter, and most have experienced several betrayals at the hands of their superiors. If you do not care, many of them will not. Some of them, unknown to you, will turn out to be smarter than they let on and will go. That is why it is a totally private, confidential program. It is also why, along with using a therapist and a peer support officer for the annual squad presentations, we suggest using a retiree, preferably from another department, for added credibility.

We have asked cadet classes how many of them have seen the inside of a therapist's office prior to arrival at the academy, for anything from a family divorce to an alcoholic parent, issues of their own, or anything else. It has not been surprising to see as many as a quarter to a third of the hands go up. One of the reasons we emphasize the importance of beginning ESC training in the academy and once a year after is to reinforce this positive attitude and keep it resistant against the warrior culture that awaits them and may try to discourage it.

Veteran officers are often taken by surprise at the suggestion of seeing a therapist as a part of their routine health care. Objections and challenges are extremely rare. We forget that police officers are a well-educated part of our society and that they appreciate being approached with a program that is presented respectfully and offers intelligent choices. When this happens, they respond with curiosity and interest. Many reserve judgment, but their minds are obviously open, and one might well expect that some will take advantage of the option.

Just like suicide prevention, it will take time. Keeping officers mentally fit is as important as maintaining their physical and tactical fitness. A police officer who is preoccupied, anxious or depressed is not alert or safe. With violence and fears of terrorism increasing in our own country, it is more important than ever that we keep our officers well-trained emotionally, as well as physically and tactically. We send them through our academies, and ten years later we expect these same officers to shoot straight and not have accidents, complaints, lawsuits, patrol car accidents, grievances, or family problems.

The Financial Benefits of ESC to a Department

There is a strong correlation between employee mental health and employer costs. One study (Danna & Griffin, 1999) points out that U.S. industry loses 50 million working days annually due to stress-related absenteeism. Another study by Thomas and Hersen (2001) flatly stated that, if unabated, the stress process can produce more serious, chronic decrements, such as heart disease, chemical depression, and alcoholism.

Nowhere are these continual stressors more evident than in law enforcement. The kinds of societal costs suffered by industry as a whole are mirrored in different and often more dramatic ways in law enforcement due to the increased pressures, dangers, and public exposure. Both programs being discussed, ESC and suicide prevention, can proactively and reactively care for the individual and group's emotional well-being.

The *proactive* element, ESC, is designed for multiple purposes and true cost savings, not only those related to the dollars needed to train and replace a disability-retired or dead officer, but also the costs of maladaptive coping techniques for stress among other officers, including those who are already within the "loop" of PTSD.

One of the intended advantages of a good mental health program is to save a department money. A police chief need only look at some of the potential savings:

- Complaints of rudeness and misuse of force
- Off-duty complaints
- Lawsuits
- Alcoholism
- Grievances
- Vehicle accidents and unnecessary maintenance
- Sick leave and injury time off
- Equipment abuse
- Theft and other issues
- Divorces and other relationship problems

WHY DO WE NEED "MORE" THAN SUICIDE PREVENTION?

We need a two-pronged approach that includes both programs. ESC and suicide prevention need one another. If our mental health component fails and an officer reaches "critical mass" or becomes suicidal, we want the following to happen.

- Officers reach into their tool bag of resources they have learned in ESC training and recognize the need for help.
- The officers then reach out for help.
- If they do not, we hope the combined suicide prevention team and ESC will be able to pick up on the individual and intervene.

Choosing the Right Therapist for You

Cops do not trust easily, which makes the walk to a therapist's door seem like tiptoeing through a minefield. Once inside, a cop with twenty years on the job and nervous tics over both eyes will suddenly blurt out that "everything is fine" and dash for the door. This is why it is good to be prepared with a few clues on what to look for.

1. *"Police officers should only see therapists who are cops or know all about police work."* Sadly, many officers out there are missing some good therapy because they cannot find a "cop doc."

There are some excellent psychologists and therapists out there. Some are former police officers or, if not, have worked extensively with cops and/or police departments. Some advertise themselves as such in police publications or on the internet. Much of it depends on how you (or the police culture) wants to define "cop doc." You should not assume that the shingle alone means this is the proper therapist for you. Instead, you should follow all the criteria for selecting any therapist, which are outlined in more detail in the following.

Psychologists and therapists come in all personalities and styles. I have felt famously comfortable with one "cop doc" and not another. I have spent my longest and most fruitful time with a therapist who had worked with many PTSD patients – but not police officers. It was tremendously helpful and cathartic for me to explain my work and experiences to her (and now her practice includes many police officers).

Here is the point: a good psychologist/therapist treats *human beings*, not cops or forklift drivers.

2. *Here are some simple criteria to use if you are just beginning your search for a therapist.*

- Your therapist should be licensed to practice in your state. If he or she is *not* a mental health therapist/social worker, psychiatrist, or psychologist licensed to treat mental disorders, avoid him or her.
- Call and talk to the person. Ask some questions and see how comfortable you feel with her or him. If the therapist does not have time for you on the phone as a new client, she or he may not have time for you in an emergency.
- You should be comfortable with your therapist's style during your first visit.

- For dealing with law enforcement issues, your therapist should have experience working with job stress and PTSD patients.
- A therapist should not express shock, dismay, or begin weeping the first time you describe something disturbing.
- Lastly, it would be great if your therapist is a "cop doc." (A note: All of the previous criteria apply to your cop doc as well.)

You will probably notice more notes are taken in a first visit or two than later on. This is necessary as part of "getting to know you." Ask questions. After all, you are the client.

1. Avoid this: *"I tried therapy one time and it didn't work for me."* I went in for an initial consultation with a highly reputed back surgeon. When we shook hands, the first thing I noticed was that he had dirty fingernails. I did not go back to see him. I did not give up on seeing back surgeons, however. I found another one who met my criteria – and had clean fingernails.
2. *"The department's psychologist/Employee Assistance Plan (EAP) is just a conduit to the Chief."* It might be. Probably not, but if you're that suspicious, go out and find your own private therapist. Use your own health plan, pay the co-pay, and select a counselor you *know* is not on the chief's speed dial.

CONCLUSIONS

The challenge is whether we wish to move forward. It is a challenge we can meet if we are willing to broaden our focus from standing at the edge of the cliff with a sign that says, "Don't Jump," to a broader view of our responsibilities that includes the emotional well-being of *all* our officers – not merely those that are in trouble or feeling suicidal.

We cannot limit ourselves to preventing suicides any longer. Our responsibility is too great and too many are in need. We must take a giant step. Through implementation of an ESC training program, we can set an example for others to follow. It is time, finally, to make the emotional safety and health of all our personnel a top priority – not just by our words, but by our actions. *It is no longer just about suicide – it is about the mental health of all our officers!*

At this moment, carnage and horror are taking place in multiple cities and towns and fields across our country. We have police officers dealing with them – right now, at this moment. In a few minutes, they are going to drive away from the scene, finish their reports, and go home. Some live alone and some have to get their children off to school. Some will go to court; others have second jobs and some lead secret lives. Within a few hours, all will have "forgotten" the depravities of the night. Everything will be tucked neatly away in the distant recesses of their minds in a file named, "Nightmares." It will stay right there; ready to go, along with all the other nightmares of the last ten years.

If these officers are lucky, there will be room in the file for another ten or twenty years. None of them needs a suicide prevention program. They are not suicidal. They are not in trouble. They are quite well, thank you very much. When the time comes, they just want their pension. With it, however, will come that file.

REFERENCES

Anderson, B., & Dahlgren, E. (2002, June 26). When job stress becomes disabling. *Business Week Magazine,* 16–18.

Atkinson-Taylor, L. (2003). The impact of repeated exposure to trauma. *Law & Order, 51,* 118–124.

Bonokoski, M. (2009, February 15). Honour for cop overdue. *Toronto Sun.*

Danna, K., & Griffin, R. W. (1999). Health and well-being in the workplace: A review and synthesis of the literature. *Journal of Management, 25,* 357–384.

Dahl, J. (2009, January 24). The police suicide problem. *Boston Globe.*

McCann, I. L., & Pearlman, L. A. (1990). Vicarious traumatization: A framework the psychological effects of working with victims. *Journal of Traumatic Stress, 3,* 131–149.

Robinson, H. M., Sigman, M. R., & Wilson, J. P. (1997). Duty-related stressors and PTSD symptoms in suburban law enforcement officers. *Psychological Reports, 81,* 835–845.

Thomas, J. C., & Hersen, M. (2001). *Psychopathology in the workplace: Recognition and adaptation* (pp. 293–311). New York: Brunner-Routledge.

Violanti, J. M. (2007). *Police suicide: Epidemic in blue* (2nd ed.). Springfield, IL: Charles C Thomas.

Chapter 7

SURVIVORS: THE PERSONAL TRAGEDY OF POLICE SUICIDE

Teresa T. Tate

It is important that we honor every law enforcement officer who died while serving his or her community. The manner of their death does not determine the value of their service.

President Obama

Each year, more than 33,000 Americans die by suicide. The suicide rate among military soldiers has steadily increased since 2006, with the majority of the suicides happening at home in the United States. Law enforcement suicides are not always reported, and inaccuracies have occurred, leaving the question of just how many officers die by suicide compared to line-of-duty deaths.

When a suicide occurs, there is a ripple effect that reaches not only the officer's immediate family, but his peers and the community as well. For every suicide, there are at least six immediate family members affected by the death. Add the police family, and you can multiply that number by five: the officer's squad, dispatchers, and the officers working in the assigned precinct who may overlap the shift.

Mental health professionals believe that the mourning experience for survivors of suicide is more intense and complicated than any other type of death. They experience a sudden and unexplainable death compounded with the aftermath associated with the stigma of mental illness and suicide. They experience emotions such as profound sadness, shock, anger, guilt, shame, rejection, anxiety, and confusion. Even those survivors who were completely surprised by the act of suicide are known to agonize over the fact that they were unable to prevent the suicide. There is no time frame for a survivor of suicide to recover from this loss, and in fact, their grief may be long term. In essence, survivors must learn to cope with their loss, while knowing there will be no closure. The brother of a widow claimed that when her husband pulled the trigger, he gave her a life sentence. A loved one's suicide causes a pain that never completely goes away and a heart that will never truly mend. It is a death that has more questions than answers. One of the hardest aspects of suicide is accepting the fact that the family may never know why it happened. Part of the grief process is to let go of asking the question "Why?" Survivors, as well the officer's coworkers, tend to replay the last days of the officer's life, searching for clues or trying to understand their state of mind.

Police officers need answers as well. If officers are unable to understand why the act occurred, they tend to shift their focus on the family, which inevitably brings about blame. Numerous newspaper articles have been written immediately after an officer suicide in which the chief or sheriff publicly states that the officer was having marital problems. By deflecting the blame away from the police department and onto the family, administrators have, in essence, retreated from the family. A more compassionate way of handling the media would be to say, "We are saddened to have lost an officer to suicide. Our hearts and prayers are with the officer's family." Although you cannot lessen a survivor's loss, it is important that you do not add to it.

There are media reporting guidelines on several national suicide prevention organizations' websites. Respectable reporting should take the place of speculation and innuendo, and administrators and officers should avoid fueling inaccurate reporting by limiting their quotes or speaking on anonymity. Police administrators who publicly place blame on the family inflict additional and unnecessary pain onto the survivors.

For most people who have not been affected by suicide, the word "suicide" has no painful meaning. Dine in any restaurant and you are likely to find a dessert called "suicide by chocolate" or a degree of hot sauce labeled as "suicide." Things of this nature or jokes about suicide perpetuate the stigma and misunderstanding of suicide. It creates more pain to those who have been affected by suicide. Have you ever heard of "cancer cake" or "cardiac cookie?" Would you even consider buying a dessert with that name? So why do businesses, as well as society in general, think that the word "suicide" should be thought of as delectable or adventurous?

POSTTRAUMATIC STRESS DISORDER

In the aftermath of a police suicide, it has become common among survivors, predominantly spouses, to be diagnosed with PTSD. PTSD is an anxiety disorder that can develop after exposure to trauma, a threatening situation, or physical harm. In these cases, the onset of PTSD is generally attributed to witnessing the act of suicide by their loved one or to being the family member who discovers the officer's body.

Survivors who have PTSD may feel stressed or frightened even if they are no longer in danger. Words, objects, or situations that remind the survivor of the event can trigger nightmares, flashbacks, or frightening thoughts.

The secondary trauma that may be inflicted on family members can increase the intensity of PTSD. This trauma is caused by either the responding police department or the department in which the officer was employed. In some cases, multiple jurisdictions may be involved. The additional trauma that the survivor may experience are gunpowder residue tests; evidence of blood on the hands, face, or clothing of the survivor; restricted access to the officer's body; and insensitive behavior from other officers. In cases in which responding officers collect the survivor's clothing as evidence, it would be appropriate to allow the survivor to change clothing at the home and then surrender the soiled clothing. It is inexcusable behavior for any officer to escort a survivor to the police station in clothing that is soiled with physical evidence from the officer.

In some cases, the secondary trauma may actually begin with the 911 dispatcher. Dispatchers are trained to assist the caller in trying to save a life until an emergency medical technician (EMT) arrives; however, it becomes traumatic when dispatchers expect the family member, after witnessing the act, to render life-saving measures to an officer who has shot himself or herself in the heart or the head. Survivors tell the stories of dispatchers instructing them to perform cardiopulmonary resuscitation (CPR) on an officer with a head wound or to sit on the officer's chest and compress the entry wound with their own hands. In the cases of hanging, survivors are instructed to cut the rope in order to release the body but generally are not physically able due to the weight of the officer, as well as the accessibility of the rope.

Over time, survivors learn that certain noises, such as fireworks, gunshots, sirens, or medical television shows that depict bloody scenes, can trigger a physical or emotional response. Reactions to these noises can include flashbacks, hyperventilating, crying, nightmares, and a sense of fear. Spouses who worked in close proximity to the officer may experience anxiety attacks when having to interact with the officer's coworkers. Even babies and young children who heard the fatal gunshot and witnessed the distress of their mother or father can experience an emotional reaction, for example crying, when they are exposed to loud noises such as the phone ringing or a door bell sounding.

Survivors attempt to identify events or noises that may trigger a reaction in the form of flashbacks, nightmares, anxiety, and panic attacks. Until a trigger is experienced and identified, survivors will not know what event or sound will affect them.

> A survivor had attended a memorial service for a retired police officer decades after her husband's suicide. The retired officer was the first member of the bomb squad for a local police department in South Florida. A touching tribute of six bomb trucks from surrounding jurisdictions as well as a federal law enforcement agency were parked at the entrance of the church. That night, the survivor suffered nightmares of a police officer in uniform, gun drawn, standing at her doorway trying to gain entry into her house. Due to the secondary trauma that this survivor experienced, the impact of seeing so many law enforcement officers in one place triggered a response that she was not aware would occur.

A COMPARISON OF SURVIVOR BENEFITS

Family members of officers killed in the line of duty are entitled to a one-time federal Public Safety Officers Benefit (PSOB) of $311,810 from the Department of Justice. PSOB defines a line of duty death as "the direct and proximate result of a personal injury sustained in the line of duty."

Family members of officers who die by suicide may receive compensation from a life insurance policy if the policy was in effect for two years or more. Depending on the length of service with the department, retirement benefits may be paid either in a lump sum of the amount paid into retirement by the officer or the family may be eligible for a monthly annuity.

In March 2009, a letter was sent to President Obama alerting him to a silent epidemic that is affecting our law enforcement officers – suicide. The letter addressed several issues, including the need for suicide prevention training for all law enforcement officers, the stigma associated with suicide that is inevitably placed upon the surviving family, and the lack of survivor benefits. It also noted that there were cases of officers who died by their own hand and that the death could be directly attributed to a job-related incident that left the officer physically disabled and emotionally traumatized.

President Obama replied in a personal letter that, It is important that we honor every law enforcement officer who died while serving his or her community. The manner of their death does not determine the value of their service.

It is interesting to note that the Department of Defense and the Department of Veterans Affairs pay survivor benefits to the family of a soldier who dies while on active duty. Active duty is not defined as line of duty and therefore includes a suicide death. If the suicide occurs on or off base or after duty hours, the family is still eligible for benefits. The military will pay a one-time nontaxable death gratuity of $100,000 to survivors of a member of the armed forces who dies while on active duty. This benefit is payable to a survivor of a military suicide.

Military funeral honors, which include an honor guard detail, presentation of the American flag, and the playing of taps, are mandated by law and are eligible to a soldier who dies by suicide. A gold star lapel pin is provided to the family of service members who die while on active duty. It is a symbol of appreciation of a service member's sacrifice to our country. How ironic that the military offers a gold star, but many police departments have refrained from allowing officers to wear mourning bands across their badges in remembrance.

The purpose of presenting the survivor benefits and funeral protocol of military soldiers in comparison to law enforcement is that many active duty soldiers are never in harm's way yet they receive the same honorable recognition and tributes after their death. Law enforcement agencies should reflect on the officer's service record and honor him or her for the sacrifices made throughout his or her career. After the death of a veteran, the next of kin receives a Presidential Memorial Certificate that bears the signature of the President, expressing the Nation's grateful recognition of the veteran's service. When a law enforcement officer dies by suicide, the family is generally no longer acknowledged and, in most cases, publicly ignored and stigmatized. The difference between a military suicide and a law enforcement suicide, when it comes to survivor benefits as well as the treatment of the family, is surmountable.

Sharing the story of a family member's suicide is personal and quite painful. Gratitude is expressed to all the survivors who were willing to tell their story even though doing so opened up wounds that may never heal. To relive those last moments of a life shared can bring back haunting memories and emotional distress. Hearing their voices tremble while reliving the nightmare of witnessing their loved one ending his or her life was truly heartbreaking. Survivors should be commended for agreeing to tell their stories so that law enforcement officers and administrators not only can learn the signs that may have been exhibited, but also realize the mistakes that could have been avoided. There were also acts of compassion and sympathy shown to the surviving families, which alleviated any discord between the family and the police department. Without the courage and strength of these survivors, their stories could not be told.

Case One

A forty-eight–year-old federal agent, who had a total of fifteen years of federal law enforcement experience with two agencies, was also an Army Ranger prior to his law enforcement career. The agent held a master's degree in political science, spoke five languages, and held dual citizenship.

The agent had several profound life-changing personal events within a four-year period prior to his death. He changed agencies, relocated across the country twice, lost his only surviving parent, had major surgery, was assigned to provide investigative data support after 9/11, divorced, and remarried.

Several months prior to the agent's death, his agency was undergoing reorganization and was being absorbed by another federal agency. Part of the agent's duties as cosupervisor included personnel issues (approval of vacation/sick leave, payroll, training, etc.). In the last few months prior to his death, the agent was under extreme pressure and stress as he tried to meet an impending deadline to upgrade all personnel within his department, including himself.

Several weeks prior to his death, the agent learned that his supervisor, as well as most of the existing directors, would not be offered the newly created positions within the new agency. The director, whom the agent highly respected, announced that he would leave the agency and take an early retirement. The widow stated that the agent was devastated after learning this news and had feelings of hopelessness about his agency. The agent told his wife that a coworker had not been fulfilling his duties, leaving more work for himself. He was having difficulty taking care of his responsibilities as well as those of his coworker. The more stress the agent felt at work, the more stressed he was at home. He increasingly had mood swings and began yelling at his wife over petty things. The agent's wife tried to convince him to see a doctor or counselor, but he refused. He would not consider counseling because he was a cop. The agent suffered from several health conditions but felt that he did not have the time to address them. He was also in chronic pain from injuries suffered during his military and law enforcement careers. His widow recalls that so much of their life was out of control.

A few weeks prior to the agent's death, the agent and his wife attended a groundbreaking ceremony for a new office building. At the last minute, the agent's director assigned the task of speaking at the ceremony to the agent, which upset him tremendously. The agent felt that he did not have sufficient time to draft and prepare a speech. This task was originally assigned to his cosupervisor. While listening to his speech at the event, the widow thought that his speech was odd and almost did not fit the situation. She remembers thinking, "does anyone else see this?"

The night the agent died, he was preparing for an out-of-town assignment. The agent's wife was asking questions about his travel plans. The agent became upset and his wife exited the bedroom. When she returned to the bedroom for the night, the agent was sitting in a chair with a bag on his lap; he pulled out a gun and shot himself in front of his wife.

The widow dialed 911 and was instructed to exit the home. The widow, who was traumatized by what she witnessed, recalls crawling out of the bedroom, rolling down the stairs and attempted to exit the house through the back door. The widow was unable to find the door handle and proceeded to run out the front door, where an EMT assisted her into an ambulance. Within a short period of time, a fellow agent arrived at the home.

After being attended to by the EMT, the widow was transported via patrol car to the police station. She was given a change of clothing that was retrieved from her home, and her pajamas were collected as evidence. At the police station, she was fingerprinted and interviewed. After release from the police department, an agent from her husband's agency transported the widow to the agent's home.

The agent leaves behind a wife and extended family members.

Comments

On occasion, federal agencies undergo reorganizations during which the agency is possibly absorbed with an existing agency, reduced in size, and even disbanded. Layoffs and transfers are also a possibility. This was the reality of what was occurring for this agent who was told that he would have to reapply for his current job. It was common knowledge that the agents from the agency being absorbed were being replaced with agents from the existing agency. These agents were told that they would never be promoted higher than their current position.

The widow was so traumatized by seeing her husband die that she was unable to return to her home for a week. In order to assist the widow, the agent's coworkers entered the home to retrieve paperwork as well as the suit to bury him in. Most of the agent's coworkers attended the funeral as well as supervisors from the agency's regional office and agents from other states. The widow stated that the response from her husband's agency was friendly and kind. Five years after the agent's death, she still maintains contact with her husband's coworkers.

Although the agent's funeral was attended by a number of local law enforcement officers as well as fellow agents from other states, it should also be noted that the assigned EAP representative refused to visit the widow and provide assistance. The agency had to seek the assistance of a second EAP representative, from across the country, who was then flown in to assist the family. In hindsight, if a resource has a personal issue with a death by suicide, it is certainly better for the family to not have to deal with such a person in order to avoid additional stigma or trauma.

As most cases of law enforcement suicide will conclude, the surviving family members did not know the signs of suicide. The widow feels that if she had known, she could have provided her husband with help. Law enforcement agencies that offer EAP programs to their employees and their families need to make a conscientious effort to provide this information, not only to the employees but also to the families. The widow was not aware of the agency's EAP program and therefore did not know that resources were available to help her husband.

A couple of weeks after the funeral, an agent visited the widow and stated that he had witnessed a bizarre incident at the office a few months prior to the agent's death. Although this incident caused enough concern for the agent to question his behavior, he felt it was not anything he could report or discuss with another supervisor. Instead, he watched the agent's behavior and decided he was okay. It is possible that the agent was exhibiting signs of suicide and that neither his coworkers nor his wife were aware of what they were seeing. Without knowledge of the signs of depression, PTSD, and suicide, we tend to realize that possibly something is wrong by this change in behavior, but the thought of suicide rarely enters our minds.

The widow sought counseling immediately after her husband's suicide and was diagnosed with PTSD. She has found that when stress builds up, it causes problems for her at work and in her personal life. The aftermath of her husband's suicide has been devastating.

Case Two

A twenty-nine-year-old police officer, who had seven years' experience with two police departments, was a member of the Army military police (MP) prior to joining a local sheriff's office. At the age of twenty-two, after the death of his father, the officer learned the truth of his mother's death from his stepmother. Since childhood, the officer was unaware that his mother had died by suicide. The officer never mentioned to his wife that he was angry with his father for lying, and he tended to rationalize and make excuses for the way his father handled the truth.

Two months prior to the officer's death, his partner, who was one of his best friends, resigned from the police department and relocated to another state for a new law enforcement opportunity. The officer was sad to lose his partner and friend.

During this time, the officer and his wife were having marital issues. The couple had been in marriage counseling intermittently over a two-year period prior to his suicide. Their therapy sessions consisted of couple's counseling as well as individual counseling through the police department's EAP program. An issue between the couple was that the husband wanted to talk about his problems with his wife late at night, whereas she was tired and the timing was not always suitable. This behavior seemed to have begun when the officer started taking diet supplements for weight loss. While utilizing the EAP services for counseling, the officer's health insurance benefits changed, so the officer had to start counseling sessions with a new therapist. The officer met once on his own with the new counselor; however, he took his life prior to the second appointment.

The officer was assigned the afternoon shift, which ended at 1 AM. The officer's widow considered her husband to be a heavy drinker. After each shift, the officer and his peers would go to a police bar where the officer was the manager and drink beer. After arriving home, he would fall asleep on the sofa and not wake up until it was time to go to work. On his days off, the officer would interact with his two young children and would always end the day by drinking beer late into the night.

A few weeks prior to the officer's death, he called into work sick, which was unusual behavior for the officer. The officer never called in sick, even if he was ill. A few days after this event, the wife called his sergeant to say something was wrong and her husband needed help. The officer picked up the extension in another room and told his sergeant everything was fine. The sergeant told the wife to work it out because there was nothing that he could do. After the conclusion of the phone call, the officer became angry with his wife, which made their marital problems worse.

A few days before the officer died, he wrote a letter to his wife. He mailed the letter, and it arrived after his suicide. The officer wrote that he felt like a monster and thought his children would be better off growing up without him. He felt that his wife was afraid of him and this was the right thing for him to do.

Two days before his death, the officer's wife came home and found her husband intoxicated and the children asleep in bed. The officer handed a note to his wife and told her to read it. She saw his gun on the bed, and he told her to take the children and get out of the house. The wife grabbed the gun, and they struggled over it. The officer was able to gain control of the gun and pointed it at his wife, who covered her face in fear that he would shoot her. He wanted her to take the children and leave; however, she feared that if she left he would kill himself. The officer then fired a shot into the mattress. She woke the children and took them to a hotel. Later that morning, the officer found her at the hotel. They agreed that he would stay at a friend's house for a few days to give the wife some space. After two days, the officer convinced his friend that he was alright, but prior to leaving, the friend called the department's EAP office to ask for advice and the EAP counselor said that the officer was fine to leave. After leaving the friend's house, the officer went to a police bar and while there wrote a suicide note to his wife. After leaving the bar intoxicated, the officer drove to his house. As the officer approached the house, the wife, who was outdoors, saw him and out of fear ran into the house and locked the door. The officer pounded on the front door shouting he wanted to say goodbye to his children.

The wife called 911. The responding police officers located the officer walking down the street and after being stopped, the officer put the gun to his head. The officer worked in one police jurisdiction and lived in another jurisdiction, so the responding police officers were not aware that he was a police officer. The responding officers pointed their weapons at the officer, and the officer took his own life. The officer died at 9:03 PM. As they approached the body, the responding officers noticed the officer's badge displayed on his belt. The widow, who remained in the house, saw an ambulance and fire truck drive by and called dispatch. She was told that they had no information for her at that time. An hour after his death, the police chaplain and one of the officer's best friends came to the house to notify the wife that her husband had died by suicide. The widow wanted to go to the scene and see her husband but was not allowed to leave the home. The chief of police from the officer's department came to the house once the officer was identified as a police officer. The chief promised the spouse that she would be allowed to go to the scene and see his body prior to being removed. At 2:00 AM, five hours after the officer had taken his life, the spouse was escorted down the street where she was allowed to see the body bag that her husband was in, but she was not permitted to open it.

Since the widow was refused access to her husband, communication between the widow and the police department became tense. An officer from the police department saw a suicide note on the dash of the officer's locked truck, but the widow refused to allow the police department to have access to the note. The officer's department requested jurisdiction over the crime scene, and the local police department agreed. The officer's department obtained a search warrant to retrieve the note and towed his truck. The suicide note was written to his fellow officers apologizing for being "tough duty."

The chief of police from the officer's department did not attend the funeral, and the widow learned from the officer's friends that it was because he died by suicide. The chief authorized the officer to be buried in his uniform along with his badge, as well as permitting the officers to wear their uniforms to the funeral. Two of the officer's closest friends assisted the widow with funeral arrangements because the department did not assign a liaison officer. A twenty-one–gun salute was held at the gravesite, which caused emotional reflexes from the widow. A flag was presented to the widow due to his prior military record.

The officer leaves behind a wife and two children.

Comments

The officer's behavior had been changing over a period of time. For reasons unknown to the widow, the officer reunited with family members who resided in another state and whom he had not seen in more than twenty years.

Although the department offers EAP services to their employees for counseling and was being utilized by the officer and his wife, it was unfortunate that the department's health insurance provider changed and therefore the officer was required to begin counseling with a new therapist. This can be detrimental to anyone undergoing counseling where they may have finally built a trustful relationship with their counselor only to find they must begin anew. When establishing EAP services, departments should consider how to appropriately support an officer as he or she transitions from one therapist to another. A possible consideration would be to avoid contracting with therapists who utilize a limited choice of health insurers.

Even though the officer was seeking counseling treatment, the question remains as to why his peers and supervisors did not take steps to help this officer with his excessive drinking. Although they may not have been aware of his alcohol abuse at home, his widow stated that the officer was at the police bar constantly, even before and after work. Being the manager of the police bar was most definitely detrimental to his well-being. The only intervention the officer received was a ride home from an on-duty officer after drinking excessively one night. How can so many peers witness this behavior night after night and not consider addressing this issue?

The officer's friend had the forethought to contact the officer's EAP counselor to ask for advice in allowing the officer to return to his residence. The fact that the EAP counselor did not insist that the officer immediately visit the counselor for an evaluation was irresponsible. Although the department has an EAP program in place, it would seem that a review of their program may be essential after the suicide of this officer.

After the breakdown of communication between the widow and the police department at the scene, it was a compassionate offering of the department to provide support to the family by continuing counseling services through EAP. The widow accepted the counseling services for herself but preferred to obtain assistance for her children through a local mental health center for children. It is a known fact that police administrators walk away from the families of an officer suicide, especially if there was any conflict pertaining to blame, notification, funeral protocol, and so on.

The officer's death occurred a few days before Christmas, and it was commendable that the officer's peers held a fundraiser for the family. The officers not only raised money for the family but also provided gifts for the officer's children. Even though the chief did not attend the officer's funeral, he did not inhibit the coordination of the fundraising events.

Case Three

A twenty-eight–year-old police officer with two years experience had served in the Army prior to starting his law enforcement career. The officer and his wife had dated ten months prior to being married and were only married for eight months. At the time of the officer's death, his widow was five months pregnant.

During his two years of law enforcement service, the officer responded to several calls that he had difficulty processing (a child getting hurt or molested by a family member). The officer needed to talk to someone about what he saw but did not want to discuss his feelings with coworkers for fear of seeming weak. His widow stated that it became a personal mission to catch the perpetrators of each offense. The officer was also having a difficult time transitioning between work and home and separating the two environments. He would come home argumentative, moody, and angry. The officer's widow would question his behavior, and his response was that he argued with people all day long and did not know how to turn off the switch. His widow stated that he was not able to leave the work attitude at work.

The officer had wanted to be a police officer since he was a little boy. After a while, he became disappointed by what he witnessed and encountered on the calls he had responded to. He felt as though criminals had bigger guns than he did, and he feared being "taken out." He was not able to process that this was part of his job and to handle the various calls given to him. The officer also did not like certain aspects of the job (infidelity among his peers, the fear of being killed, entering a suspect's home). His widow believes that the officer was a perfectionist and wanted to be the best at everything he did. He did not want to hear anything negative and would take comments very personally. When things did not turn out the way he wanted, he was not able to look back and see what went wrong and how he could have done better.

Immediately after their wedding, the officer started accusing his wife of infidelity. The wife was a dispatcher for the state police and was assigned mandatory ride alongs. The officer became possessive and controlling with his wife. These signs were not visible to his wife prior to their marriage, but these insecurities seemed to appear later. The officer no longer wanted his wife to wear make up, dress in clothes that she wore prior to the marriage, or have direct contact with her son's father, and he would check her cell phone messages on a regular basis.

The officer was not one to have close social contact apart from his wife and was lonely and distant with others. He had one friend and a sister, who were both employed by the same police department as the officer. His mother lived in another country, and they did not keep in contact. His wife had only visited the officer's family three times in a ten-month period, whereas they spent every weekend with her family. The officer felt as though there was no one he could depend on.

Twenty-four hours prior to the officer's suicide, while at dinner, his wife received a text message from an unknown caller. The text message said, "hello." The officer took the phone and questioned his wife as to who sent the text. The officer made his wife text back and ask who was calling. The message was from a man that the wife dated years ago. The officer immediately accused his wife of cheating on him and became outraged, even calling her names.

The next day, the officer and his wife had a barbecue at their home. The officer bought a case of beer and several bottles of wine even though the invited family members did not drink alcohol. The officer was overheard talking to his five-year-old stepson and saying, "you need to be a good listener to your mommy and big brother to your little sister" (the unborn child). The spouse feels as though he was saying goodbye to his stepson.

During the barbecue, the officer asked his wife inappropriate questions in front of members of her family, attempting to get an admission that she had been unfaithful. Feeling uncomfortable with his behavior, his wife and most of the other family members went to a local park; the officer stayed home. While they were gone, the officer consumed twelve beers and was acting inappropriately. A family member went to the park to say goodbye and asked if she could take the wife's young son home with her, sensing that there were problems in the marriage.

His wife returned from the park and found her husband intoxicated, crying, and listening to music in the backyard. His wife sat next to him and hugged him. She wanted to let him know that she loved him. After a few minutes, the officer pushed her away. His wife went into the house and watched him through a window. The officer then entered the house and threw a poem at his wife and made her read it. The poem was about saying goodbye. He went to another room and played Scottish bagpipe music and told his wife that the angels were calling him. As he continued to drink more alcohol, his wife would throw the drinks away. The officer continued to pace inside and outside of the house, pointing a gun to his head. At one point, he took his gun out and said, "do you want me to do this now in the backyard?" His wife never felt as though the officer would hurt her but was doing this only to scare her. The officer again entered the house looking for his wife, who was in the bathroom. His wife exited and saw her husband sitting on the closet floor with the gun in his mouth. His wife sat on the bed, and the officer made a comment that his wife would not want him to kill himself in the closet because it would dirty her clothes. He continued to make comments about which position would be most effective for shooting himself. His wife started screaming, hoping that the neighbors would hear her and call for help, because the officer kept telling her to be quiet. The wife reached for her purse and said that she was leaving to pick up her son. The officer started to cry and was calling his wife terrible names and said that she did not want him with her. As she walked out of the bedroom door, the officer reached in his pocket, pulled out bullets, and said to his wife, "do you know what this is?" He explained that hollow point bullets could cause major damage to the body. As his wife turned to leave, he told her not to leave because if she did, she would not like what she saw when she returned. His wife told her husband to put the gun away, and she would return to the room to talk to him. He agreed, but when she reentered the room, his wife noticed the gun sticking out from under the sofa. As she turned around to leave, she heard the gunshot. His wife attempted to call 911, but the officer had unplugged all the phones in the house.

Because the officer lived in one jurisdiction and worked in another, the local police department handled the investigation of the officer's suicide. A sergeant from the officer's police department arrived but never approached the widow. The sergeant was only there to retrieve police property (badge, firearm, laptop, and Taser).

The wife was transported to the local police department and was subjected to a gunpowder residue test of her hands, photographing of her face and hands, and testing of her clothing. The investigating police department provided updates of the officer's condition to his wife while she was being questioned. She was released from the police department and arrived at the hospital twenty minutes after the officer died.

Five days after the officer's death, he was cremated and buried without the widow being present. The officer's sister claimed that she had power of attorney for the officer and told the widow that they would plan the funeral with the widow's input with the arrangements. The widow was unaware that his family had plans to bury the officer without her being present. The day after the funeral, the officer's family held a memorial service. There was a photo display that had pictures of the officer and his past girlfriends. Family members, who spoke at the service, spoke only of his life prior to their marriage. There was no mention of the officer's widow and their unborn child.

The officer leaves behind a wife and two young children.

Comments

It was unfortunate for the family that the officer neglected to change the beneficiary information after marrying his wife. With regard to survivor's benefits, the widow received the amount of money that the officer had contributed to his retirement as well as a life insurance policy. The officer had not completely changed his beneficiary information on all his benefit forms and therefore his sister received payment on a union life insurance policy.

Although the officer's sister is employed by the same police department, she knowingly provided false information about the couple. This was learned after the memorial service when the widow contacted the police department to retrieve her husband's personal property. While there, she volunteered information about the officer's life to clear up rumors that his sister was spreading. The police department admitted that they accidentally released his personal property to his sister, who claimed that the officer and the spouse were divorced.

Much can be said about the dysfunction of families during times of crisis and stress. However, families have a tendency to pull apart and place blame on the widow when a suicide has occurred. Not only was the widow excluded from the burial of her husband, but she was also purposely unacknowledged at the memorial service. Several months later, the widow discovered that the officer's sister did not have power of attorney, but in fact the document that she purportedly had was actually a medical directive. Although the officer's sister resides nearby, she has not made any attempts to see the officer's baby since she was born. Based on the actions of the sister, as well as comments from the widow, it appears that the officer's sister blames the widow for the officer's suicide. Even though the sister was amicable to the widow during the few times they interacted while the couple was married, the sibling's relationship was more distant than close, with the sister telephoning sporadically with updates on relatives. Although the siblings had the opportunity to see each other at work, they did not spend time together off the job.

The only contact that the widow has had with the police department was on the one-year anniversary of the officer's death. The widow received a call from a captain on the police department who said, "If there was anything that I could do different, I would." The widow asked if the police department had developed any programs to help officers who may be dealing with stress or suicidal thoughts. She also requested whether she could receive counseling through the department's EAP program because she no longer had health insurance. Approximately two months passed without any response from the department. It was not until the widow contacted the captain that she learned the department authorized five visits to a therapist through the EAP office. If the department is going to contact the family and ask if they need assistance, they should be cognizant in responding to the family in an appropriate amount of time.

Case Four

A thirty-one–year-old police officer with more than three years experience in a local police department had been depressed since he was approximately nineteen years old. The officer was not diagnosed and treated for depression until his midtwenties. When he was seventeen years old, the officer lost his best friend in a car accident in which he was a passenger in the vehicle. Within a few years, his grandparents, his father, and his half brother died as well. During high school, he also suffered severe injuries to his jaw during a bicycle accident that prevented him from eating, speaking, or attending school for six months.

While applying for a position as a police officer in the community where he grew up, he divulged on the application that he was under psychiatric treatment and included a letter from his psychiatrist that he was fit for duty. The police department had their own mental health professional interview the officer as well as conduct a psychological assessment prior to his being offered employment. Although the officer was taking antidepressant medication, he suffered minor bouts of depression over time. The officer graduated the police academy with honors and received two out of three awards in his class. The awards were for the highest grade point average and the top gun award.

At the end of each shift, the officer would come home and process the day's incidents with his wife. His wife, who is a social worker, would suggest resources that were available in the community so that he could offer help to citizens when he responded to calls. His wife always told him that he had the mind of a police officer but the heart of a social worker.

Within the first year of being a police officer, he was promoted to a field training officer. This new assignment brought on added responsibility and stress for the officer. A year later, his wife started to see the first signs of depression after three hurricanes hit the local area within a short period of time. The police department required the officers to work twenty-four–hour shifts and sleep at the police station. During the storms, the officer's wife chose to be evacuated from the area, because she was eight months pregnant. These circumstances added to the officer's stress.

During this two-month time frame of storms, the officer spoke to his wife about suicide. At one point, the officer agreed that he was too overwhelmed with responsibility and decided to take a medical leave of absence so that he could admit himself into a hospital for a psychological evaluation and treatment. The couple began the process by obtaining a signed medical leave of absence form from the officer's personal psychiatrist. Once the officer had seen his psychiatrist and obtained the paperwork, he told his wife that he no longer felt suicidal but felt relieved that he did not have to immediately return to work. The officer took a medical leave of absence for four to five weeks and decided against checking himself into the hospital. During his medical leave of absence, his psychiatrist changed his medication, and he continued with his weekly counseling sessions. Although the officer admitted to his superiors that he was stressed and depressed, he did not tell them that he had thoughts of suicide. His department was supportive, understanding, and sympathetic toward his request for medical leave, but he was relieved of his duty weapon, badge, and patrol car. When the officer returned to work, he had a fresh attitude and was well-rested.

Within a few weeks of returning to duty, the officer was allowed to take another four weeks of personal leave to be home with his wife and newborn baby. For the next nine months, the officer struggled with his depression. The officer told his wife how important it was for him to be well for his child. He was always cognizant of his mental wellness and working to battle his depression. His efforts to overcome his illness included weekly counseling sessions, medication management, talks with his pastor, daily prayer, eating a healthy diet, exercise, the abstinence of alcohol, reading self-motivational books, and the participation in a home behavior modification program for depression that consisted of keeping a journal, completing workbooks, and listening to tapes. Although the officer was doing everything he could to overcome his depression, he did not seem to be getting any relief, and his feelings of hopelessness began to worsen.

The week before the officer died, he had threatened to take his life approximately three or four times. During each episode, he had his gun out, but his wife had always been able to talk him out of completing the act. She never thought he would actually end his life because afterward, they would talk about his feelings. He told her he could never kill himself because he would not want to leave her and his baby. Furthermore, he was afraid of the physical pain of shooting himself, and he did not want to hurt his mother, who had already lost a son, his half brother.

While the officer's wife was getting ready for work, the officer stated he did not want to go to work. His wife told the officer that if he was staying home, the baby would remain at home with him and would not be taken to childcare. The couple began to argue. The officer ran to their bedroom and pulled out his gun. His wife followed and, once again, talked to her husband until he no longer wished to end his life. When the officer left the bedroom to feed the baby, his wife hid all the firearms in the house and nervously left for work.

When the wife arrived at work, she called her mother and the officer's sister for support and guidance. They decided that he should seek professional treatment, and both the officer's sister and mother-in-law agreed to come to the house that day to help talk the officer into admitting himself to the hospital. Once everyone was at the home, the officer became angry and was reluctant to go to the hospital, but eventually he consented. To avoid the possibility of running into fellow officers at the hospital, his wife drove the officer to a hospital in another town. During the drive, the officer became highly agitated in the car and said he would never forgive his wife for doing this. After he admitted himself voluntarily for psychiatric treatment, he broke down emotionally and stated that he was overwhelmed with life and the death of his friend and family members.

The officer was kept in the emergency room for hours and was not admitted into the psychiatric unit until the middle of the night. Because he was admitted on the weekend, there was no interaction with a psychiatrist until the next day and no group therapy sessions for two days. The admitting doctor prescribed an antipsychotic medication without the knowledge or consent of the officer's regular psychiatrist. The officer was very angry for being hospitalized and did not want his wife to visit him; however, she did see him briefly on the second day. The officer was discharged on the morning of the third day after he repeatedly told the doctor that he was no longer suicidal. He was discharged and released in his sister's care and driven home.

When the officer arrived home, he was greeted by his mother-in-law and his baby. The mother-in-law observed that he was pacing the room and did not look well. When the wife returned home from work an hour later, he expressed to her that he was anxious about returning to work and how he would explain his three-day absence. At his wife's suggestion, the couple rested in their bedroom. Although the guns remained hidden in the house, the wife was also careful to hide the keys to the patrol car parked outside because a shotgun was kept in the trunk. Unbeknownst to the wife, the officer had a second set of keys in a shirt pocket in another room. The officer was unable to relax or rest and left the room. He told his wife that he wanted to go for a drive, and he retrieved the keys to his patrol car. His wife, carrying the baby, followed him outside and questioned him as to what he was doing. The officer did not respond but opened the trunk and retrieved the shotgun. As his wife begged him to go inside to talk, he began pacing in the driveway, still holding the shotgun. The officer kept saying, "Get away from me, get away from me." He then walked into the backyard while his wife pleaded with him to put the gun down. His wife stated that her thought process was to get the shotgun away from him, but she realized that this would be dangerous for herself and her baby, who was still in her arms. She watched as her husband sat down on the ground and placed the shotgun at his chest. His wife placed the baby on the grass and within seconds, he shot himself in the chest. His wife screamed for help and then rushed to her husband to cover his wound with her hands in an effort to control the bleeding. Her mother called 911 and then came outside to begin CPR.

The police officers who responded to the scene were all fellow officers and supervisors, because the officer lived and worked in the same community. Many officers were reportedly crying and more arrived when they heard what happened. Prior to leaving her home, it was requested that the widow allow access to her home to retrieve the officer's badge, firearms, uniforms, and vest. The widow denied the officers access because she would not be there to escort them. The officers politely agreed to wait until she returned. The widow was not questioned at the scene, but instead followed the ambulance to the hospital in a patrol car. The police department agreed to interview the widow at her mother's home, an hour away, the following afternoon. The interview was very short, and the officers were respectful and remorseful.

Several hundred people, including many law enforcement officers from various jurisdictions, attended the officer's funeral. The mayor recognized the officer's duty to his community and publicly gave his condolences. The chief of police advised that any officer was welcome to attend the funeral in uniform if they chose. The widow recalls seeing police officers standing at every street corner from the church to the cemetery saluting the hearse as it passed.

The officer leaves behind his wife, son, mother, three sisters, and a brother.

Comments

The death of this officer deeply affected the members of the police department who were unaware of his battle with mental illness. Although it would seem that this officer tried valiantly to overcome this illness, it was an illness that seemed to perpetuate with the stress of the job as well as his personal life. The couple had decided that the wife would take a year off from work after the birth of their baby, but the concept of being the sole financial supporter for his family, as well as having a career and paying a mortgage seemed to overwhelm him. This was compounded further with his last voluntarily admission in the hospital without the knowledge of the top administrators of the police department. The officer was concerned that he would lose his job once the chief learned of this action as well as the taking of prescribed medication, which he was worried might interfere with his thought process at work.

Upon the officer's release, the hospital was responsible for setting up an immediate appointment with the officer's psychiatrist. A hospital employee left a message on the answering machine without following up to ensure the officer had an actual appointment. It will never be known if this mistake could have prevented the officer's suicide.

The police department's victim advocate initiated contact upon the widow's return from the hospital after the death of the officer. She maintained daily contact with the widow and provided her with resources for SOS groups and benefits and assisted her with the funeral arrangements. Monetary donations, as well as baby clothing and toys were collected by the police department and provided to the family.

The chief showed the family much compassion and respect after the death of this officer. At the request of the widow, he prevented the media from approaching the officer's house. He personally contributed a donation in memory of the officer for a national fundraiser on suicide prevention (www.afsp.org) as well as presenting the officer's badge in lucite casing to the widow during roll call training. He stated during the presentation that the widow "will always be part of our family."

The officer's counselor offered the widow free counseling service for one year. It should also be noted that the cemetery generously provided the widow the plot and headstone for free, which is generally reserved for a line-of-duty death.

Case Five

A forty-four–year-old sergeant with ten years of law enforcement service had been widowed seven years prior to his death. The sergeant, who had only been with the sheriff's department for one year, was the first deputy on the scene of a car accident involving his first wife. His attempts to revive her after her car plunged into an icy river were unsuccessful.

The sergeant and his current wife, a corrections officer, met at a local gym approximately six weeks after his wife died. He held several positions within the sheriff's department, including detective, field training officer, hostage/crisis negotiator, and sergeant at arms for the police union. Throughout his career, the sergeant had received numerous awards and commendations. He was also the sheriff's campaign manager and trusted friend. His widow stated that he was very well-respected and seemed to be everyone's confidant.

Approximately two years prior to his suicide, the sergeant was involved in a line of duty shooting. The sergeant, as well as other deputies involved in the incident, received a plaque from the sheriff's department as well as being awarded the Deputy of the Year. His widow stated that her husband was aloof in discussing how he felt about the shooting and would not describe his emotions. Instead, he would describe how the other deputies responded and how the situation could have been handled differently.

The year before his death, the sergeant was selected to participate in an interagency drug enforcement detail with the FBI. This also included his attending training at the FBI Academy in Quantico, Virginia, and being away from home for lengthy time periods. Part of his assignment on the detail was to work undercover on a gang task force.

Because the couple both had careers in law enforcement, it was a normal practice to discuss the day's events with each other at home. When his wife left her position as a corrections officer after the birth of their first child, they still maintained this practice. However, his wife began to see his behavior change when he started the FBI detail, and it was at this point that he stopped telling his wife about his work assignments. He began to internalize his feelings, and his reason for not discussing work was for the safety of his wife and child.

During the sergeant's employment, he was on and off the night shift. He began to gain weight and, due to the shift work, he was unable to find the time to work out. He was also having difficulty sleeping during the day, and his wife found him sitting in the dark, drinking into the morning hours on several occasions. His wife began seeing him slip in and out of depression. A man who once was always there for everyone began to feel overwhelmed with the concept of being the confidant and advisor for so many. He commented to his wife that he was "tired of being everyone's daddy."

Eight weeks before the sergeant's death, a neighbor's daughter, who was a highway patrol sergeant, died by suicide. His widow recalls his commenting that those who were going to do it were not going to talk about it.

A week prior to the sergeant's suicide, his wife was out of town at a business conference. The couple hired a sixteen-year-old babysitter to be at the house while she was away and her husband was attending a meeting with the sheriff. When the wife returned home four days later, her husband was excited about his new duties in the department.

The next day, the sergeant repeatedly entered the house to say goodbye to his wife prior to leaving for work. Later that day, his wife took the children to the aquarium and upon returning home, she noticed that her husband was not there, his car was gone, and the television was on. She tried to call her husband on his cell phone but never received an answer nor did he return her call, which was unusual. An hour later, she received a phone call from a nearby police department asking her to identify herself and whether she knew the whereabouts of her husband. A few minutes later, the mother of the babysitter called the wife and stated that while the wife was out of town, there was inappropriate behavior between the husband and the babysitter, and she was filing a complaint. Soon after, the sheriff arrived at the house and questioned the wife as to where her husband might be and where his favorite places were and stated that he was not answering any of the phone calls. During his disappearance, the sergeant called a friend, but left a message when he was not able to reach him. The next day, the sergeant called his wife and stated that he made a mistake and that he was sorry. He also said that she should cut him loose and to take care of the children. This was the last call he made.

For the next two days, the police and FBI looked for the sergeant. Five felony warrants had been issued for his arrest. During these two days, the wife learned that the FBI had tapped her phone. This was revealed when the FBI called the friends who had called the sergeant's home for identification purposes. The media had also claimed residency outside the sergeant's home.

On the third day after his disappearance, the sergeant's partner and a lieutenant in the sheriff's department came to the home and notified the wife that they had found the sergeant's body in another state. He had obtained a cash advance from his credit card, over half of which was found in his coat. He also left a three-page letter to his wife, a letter to the police department apologizing for the mess, and a letter to his lieutenant.

The Sheriff permitted deputies to wear their class A uniforms to the memorial service. However, a few deputies refused and therefore chose not to attend the service. The Sheriff also told the widow that she would always be part of the family, but shortly after, she stated, everyone disappeared.

At the service, the district attorney spoke to the widow and stated that the report from the babysitter's father provided no information to substantiate a sexual assault. He also stated to the widow that the most that would have happened to him was that he would have lost his job, but no felony charges would have been filed. The district attorney stated that he had to file the felony charges to keep the sergeant from fleeing and to extradite him from wherever he was found.

The sergeant leaves behind a wife and three children.

Comments

It should be noted that when the sergeant's first wife died, the sheriff's department took the right approach by requiring mandatory time off, with counseling, for six weeks. After the six-week period, a psychologist cleared the sergeant fit for duty, and he returned to his duties on patrol. His widow feels that the combination of finding his first wife in the river, which brought about PTSD, the loss of the family connection with his first wife's parents upon their death, and the accusation of the babysitter was more than he could emotionally bear. He was also feeling tired, malaise, and physically unfit, which may have added to his emotional distress.

Throughout their marriage, the sergeant would experience moodiness from December through February. For many people, the holidays can be a depressing time, but it also happened to correlate to the time frame of the death of his first wife. He would talk, in detail, of how he had attempted to resuscitate his wife after the accident. His current wife would give him time and space to work out his feelings. The sergeant maintained a loving relationship with his deceased wife's parents, and he continued to mourn their loss after they died. After their death, he would talk about how the remaining family members had shut him out of the family, which deeply hurt him. The sergeant and his first wife had been childhood sweethearts, and they had all been part of each other's family for more than twenty years.

The sheriff's department provided mandatory counseling for all employees after the death of the sergeant. It is the policy and procedure within the department that debriefings are to be held after line of duty shootings, child abuse cases, and major incidents.

The sheriff's department also provided the widow psychological counseling through the department's EAP office after the death of her husband. Unfortunately, the referred counselors did not have the proper experience in dealing with the aspects of grief associated with a loss to suicide. In fact, one counselor tried to compare her own grief regarding the death of her dog to the widow's grief of losing her husband to suicide. During this initial counseling session, the widow spent her time offering the counselor a box of tissues. EAP services must ensure that the counselors with whom they have a contract have the knowledge and skills for handling specific issues associated with law enforcement and/or suicide.

The widow eventually sought psychological counseling on her own to deal with the issues of grief, the treatment she was receiving from the community, the media, and how to help her young children through their own grief.

Although the family has since relocated, the widow still maintains a friendship with a few people from the department. It is comforting to know that his friends have not forgotten him and that they continue to think about him and miss him.

Case Six

A twenty-eight–year-old traffic homicide investigator with six years of law enforcement service had been experiencing financial and marital problems for more than a year prior to his suicide. The investigator's home had been in the foreclosure process a few years prior to his suicide. His grandmother provided financial assistance to the investigator in order to save the home. Even though the investigator was working a second job, not related to law enforcement, the financial strain was continuous.

Approximately two years prior to his death, the investigator responded to the scene of a seven-year-old girl who drowned. The death of this young child affected the investigator deeply. A few months after this incident, while the investigator was at home with his young children, his own fourteen-month-old daughter fell into a bucket filled with water and almost drowned. The investigator was able to resuscitate his daughter by performing CPR, and she was then airlifted to a nearby hospital. His child was in the hospital for more than one month, and his mother stated that he always felt responsible for the accident.

As time progressed, the investigator's mother began to notice that her son was disassociating himself from her as well as his sister. She learned that the couple had been talking about getting a divorce and that her daughter-in-law had been threatening to withhold visitation of the children if he were to divorce her. Every time the mother asked her son what was wrong, he always replied, "I'm okay, mom." Even though she could tell that something was wrong, her son would never talk about his problems.

Unbeknownst to the mother, the investigator's wife had told her father-in-law that she believed her husband was suicidal. The father-in-law did not relay this information to anyone else because he and his ex-wife had always believed their daughter-in-law to be untruthful and responsible for causing a rift between the investigator and his parents.

Approximately two months prior to his death, the investigator's wife had initiated the process of having him detained under the Baker Act twice within a one-month period. Although the investigator's father was aware of his son being involuntarily detained, his mother was unaware that this had occurred until after her son's death. Years later, she still does not know why her son was detained, even after asking his wife for an explanation.

One week prior to the investigator's death, his mother visited him at his home. She recalled that the officer sat on the sofa and looked detached, as if he was observing his mother at a distance. She compared his demeanor to watching a scene but not being part of it physically.

On the evening of the investigator's death, while the children were not at home, the couple had an argument. Although alcohol was not a major factor of the investigator's state of mind, he had consumed two or three beers in the course of the evening. During the argument, the investigator's wife claimed he became angry and punched a television set, breaking his hand. The investigator's wife had walked into their bedroom when she heard the gunshot.

The deputy chief and a lieutenant from her son's department as well as two other officers from the police department in her jurisdiction notified the mother of her son's death at her residence. The following day, a meeting was held at the police department with the chief; chaplain; and the investigator's mother, sister, wife, and wife's mother. The police department coordinated and paid for the investigator's funeral, except for the gravesite, which was donated. The chief permitted an honor guard, the wearing of mourning badges, and for the investigator to be buried in his uniform. It was also permitted for officers attending the funeral to wear their uniforms. More than 500 family members, friends, police officers, and dignitaries attended the funeral. At the conclusion of the funeral, a last call transmission over the police radio was broadcast.

The investigator is survived by his mother, sister, wife, three children, and grandparents.

Comments

The Baker Act allows for involuntary examination or involuntary commitment in a local hospital or crisis unit. It can be initiated by judges, law enforcement officials, physicians, or mental health professionals. There must be evidence that the person has a mental illness or is a harm to self or others or is self-neglectful. The involuntary examinations may last up to seventy-two hours (Wikipedia, 0000).

Although the investigator was unwilling to talk to his parents about his financial and marital problems, he had attempted to make several appointments to meet with the police chaplain but could never coordinate a date. Shortly after the death of the investigator, the chaplain resigned from the police department.

The mother still has many unanswered questions as to why her son took his life. Although she was aware of the couple's problems, she was never privy to the extent of his unhappiness. The mother continues to question how her son could have had a broken hand at the time of his death, refusing to believe that he put his fist through the television. She maintains that he was a nonviolent person, who was very loving and carefree and violent behavior was not in his character.

The mother stated that the widow sued the police department for the death of her son. The department was aware that the investigator had been examined involuntarily twice in an one-month period and therefore was placed on administrative duty and relieved of his weapon. The basis of the lawsuit was that the department released the investigator from administrative duty and returned his firearm too soon. The investigator took his life approximately one month later. The widow was awarded a six-figure settlement.

Due to the blame that the investigator's mother placed on the wife immediately after her son's death, the wife prevented her from seeing the grandchildren for approximately six months. The mother had, in essence, lost her son and grandchildren at the same time. It took time for the daughter-in-law and mother to rebuild their relationship, which is a healthier one today.

Four years after the officer's suicide, three officers from the police department, as well as the officer's mother, attended the In Harm's Way: Law Enforcement Suicide Prevention conference. The police department paid the travel expenses for the mother as well. After returning from the conference, they presented the material in four three-hour inservice training courses to all sworn officers, as well as civilian personnel. Every member of the police department, with the exception of the chief of police, attended the training. Police administrators must realize that their actions do not go unnoticed and that not only do they set an example, but also a silent message of noncompliance sets them apart from the officers. Administrators must also partake in prevention and awareness training if they expect their officers to utilize the program.

Case Seven

A thirty-five–year old state trooper with thirteen years experience was also a training officer and the president of the police union. He was the recipient of numerous awards, including a Distinguished Service Award and the Trooper of the Year Award from Mothers Against Drunk Drivers. The trooper worked four ten-hour shifts each week, as well as numerous hours of overtime. He worked the night shift (6:30 PM–4:30 AM) most of his law enforcement career. The trooper suffered from sleep deprivation due to the amount of extra work hours as well as being the caretaker of his young children while his wife was at work.

Approximately two weeks prior to the trooper's suicide, he stopped two men who were walking on a road. These two individuals played a significant role in the events that led to the trooper's suicide. While approaching the men, the trooper noticed that their clothing was very dirty. There appeared to be blood on one of the men, who also had a black eye. It was possible they had been involved in an assault or a murder. The widow stated that the trooper felt that something had happened to someone that night.

During the arrest of one of the suspects, the trooper called dispatch to check the status of a firearm. The widow was told that the trooper inadvertently relayed the serial number incorrectly to the dispatcher, transposing two numbers, but he provided the correct serial number on the second relay. The widow does not know who made that mistake, but the serial number was not entered into the computer correctly and therefore the firearm was not registered as stolen. If the number had been entered in the database correctly, it would have been determined to be a stolen firearm. The trooper did not learn of this error until the day of his suicide.

The trooper arrested one suspect for possessing a concealed weapon. This weapon was confiscated by the trooper at the time of the suspect's arrest. The suspect was bailed out of jail several hours later. Approximately two weeks later, a bank robbery occurred involving the same two suspects and three additional suspects. Five people were killed during the bank robbery, and the suspects fled the scene in a stolen vehicle.

During the bank robbery, the trooper was home while his wife was running errands on her way to work. Because a street close to the bank was cordoned off, the wife contacted her husband on her cell phone to ask what was happening. The trooper and his wife, who was listening to a public radio station at the time, learned at that moment of the bank robbery. Periodically, the trooper would call in at work to learn of the new developments of the investigation. Because the trooper had to work the nightshift later that evening he did not report into work early.

When the trooper's wife arrived at home, the trooper was leaving for work and had just learned the identity of the apprehended bank robbers. The trooper told his wife that if he had been given more information and a description of the suspects earlier during the day, he would have been able to identify them from that earlier stop. The trooper realized that two of the bank robbery suspects, one of whom he arrested for carrying a concealed weapon, were the suspects he encountered two weeks prior to the robbery.

The trooper finished his shift in the early morning hours and went home. His wife waited as long as possible to wake him prior to leaving for work at a local store. The wife took their four-year-old daughter with her to work so her husband could sleep, leaving the two-year-old son in his care at home. The trooper's wife did not have a chance to discuss the situation of the bank robbery prior to leaving the house for work. The trooper's wife called him at home around midmorning, but the trooper stated that he could not talk and had to go to the office. The trooper took his two-year-old son with him. When he arrived at the office, the trooper was informed that the serial number he had reported in the incident two weeks prior had been relayed incorrectly. At this point, he was told that the firearm had been stolen.

It was determined later that the firearm that the trooper confiscated from the suspect two weeks earlier was not the weapon used in the bank robbery. However, it was subsequently discovered to be one of many weapons that were stolen at the same time as the weapon that was used in the bank robbery. After learning this, the trooper was noticeably upset. The captain asked the trooper if he wanted someone to talk to. The trooper declined and said that he wanted to talk to his wife. The trooper's wife was a part time dispatcher for the same department where the trooper was employed. The trooper left the office with his son and went home.

The trooper called dispatch upon leaving the house again, knowing that he was calling in on a recorded line, and instructed certain people to come get his wife at her store. The trooper told the dispatcher to tell his wife that her son needed her and she needed to get home. The trooper kept repeating to the dispatcher that "his job was to help people, not to hurt them." The dispatcher talked to the trooper for awhile, and he finally told the dispatcher where he was. The first responder on the scene arrived approximately ten to fifteen minutes later, but the trooper was dead. Because of the trooper's location, it would have taken some time to find him if he had not told the dispatcher where he was.

An undercover female officer arrived at the wife's store, and the wife was told to leave with the officer. The wife recalls that the police radio was turned down so she could not hear the radio traffic. The female officer drove the wife toward her home but stopped at a parking lot where a lieutenant met them. The lieutenant approached the unmarked patrol car and told the trooper's wife that her husband had killed himself. The trooper's wife had her four-year-old daughter sitting on her lap when the lieutenant said this through the open car window. After arriving at her home, she found a dispatcher and another employee inside waiting for her. The baby was found asleep in the crib. The wife stated that that these people were not considered friends but were more like work associates. The wife kept asking where her husband was, but no one would tell her. The trooper's sixteen-year-old-son had heard on the local radio that something had happened to his father prior to arriving home from school. Upon arriving home, he walked into the chaos of being a survivor of suicide.

Later that day, the trooper's captain, lieutenant, colonel, and governor came to the house to pay their respects to the trooper's widow. Representatives from another troop area came to assist with the press releases, protection from the media for the family, counseling support, as well as funeral arrangements. The visitation was restricted to family and patrol. The following day, a full police funeral was provided. The police agency complied with every request of the trooper's widow regarding funeral arrangements, even releasing balloons at the cemetery. Thousands of law enforcement officers attended the trooper's funeral, including the governor, who spoke at the funeral.

After the death of the trooper, the colonel asked how he could help the trooper's widow. For a period of six months, the colonel would call the widow to inquire how she was doing. The widow, who was working as a temporary part-time dispatcher, asked to be a permanent part-time employee so she could receive health benefits for herself and her children. When the widow returned to work, she had to apply for this new position along with other applicants. At this point, other employees felt she was getting preferential treatment and a hostile work environment emerged. Rumors were circulating implying that the widow was having an affair with a captain. She was called into the captain's office and questioned as if she was aware of the rumors circulating at the agency. When she was told this, she was not only hurt, but also bewildered as to why such untruthful statements would be said about her. A disgruntled dispatcher would talk about the widow at work as if she was not even in the room. This dispatcher continued to harass the widow during work hours. The widow sought a counselor to help her deal with the hostile work environment. The widow was not allowed to have the first anniversary date of her husband's death off from work and was told that she should work before and after support group meetings that were an hour and a half away. Because of the ongoing harassment at work, the widow resigned from her position. After this, the colonel stopped calling the widow to inquire about her well-being.

The year after the trooper's death, the widow learned that it was forbidden for troopers to visit his gravesite on Law Enforcement Memorial Day while on duty. Troopers are, however, permitted to visit the trooper's grave on their own time.

The trooper leaves behind a wife, seven children, his parents, and eight siblings.

Comments

It was a mistake for the captain to allow the trooper to leave the office after learning that the two suspects he encountered walking on the road were involved in the bank robbery. Within an hour of learning this information, the trooper took his life. Based on what the trooper repeatedly said to the dispatcher on the phone, the trooper was struggling with feeling responsible for the deaths of five people. Because the trooper showed distress after being told of the serial number error, a peer, chaplain, police administrator, EAP counselor, or a family member should have accompanied him home.

Although the law enforcement agency in this case came together as a family to help the survivors during the funeral process, it is difficult to understand why survivors are treated with menace in the same workplace as their officer. Employees working with both the law enforcement officer and the spouse, in this case dispatchers, should have been counseled in providing a work environment that is not only productive but also compassionate. Supervisors need to counsel employees who attack those who are most vulnerable. It was generous of the police union to pay the health insurance premiums for the family for three months. Because the widow left her employment as a dispatcher, her lower income status qualified her children for the school lunch program, as well as Kids Connection, a free state health insurance program for children. When you compare the death benefits of a line of duty death to a suicide death, you realize just how financially different the two deaths are classified. You will not find the children of a police officer killed in the line of duty having to apply for the free school lunch program. In fact, in many states, the children and the spouse of an officer killed in the line of duty are eligible for free college tuition.

CONCLUSION

In the cases depicted in this chapter, psychiatric disorders such as depression, alcohol abuse, and PTSD as well as genetic predisposition, in other words family history of suicide, were noted. Similarities were identified involving increasing use of alcohol, rage explosions, depression, and distress over the possibility of losing a career, all risk factors for suicide.

Police administrators may feel helpless about knowing how to support the family. It is important to honor and respect the needs of the family in the days, weeks, and months after the suicide. This can be accomplished by asking the family what help they may need.

Without a doubt, survivors need the support of their family, including the law enforcement family, and the community. Police administrators need to know that the showing of support to the family is essential to their emotional well-being. Allowing survivors access to department EAP services can provide them with a start in their support network. For many survivors, financial benefits are limited and therefore psychological counseling is not an option. Although the officer or the family may not have utilized EAP services prior to the suicide, the availability of these services should at least be extended to the immediate family. Survivors who are unable to seek counseling may be left with self-doubt, deep-seated anger, and immense guilt, which may lead to self-destructive behavior through the use of drugs, alcohol, and various social maladaptive behaviors. For those survivors who are fortunate enough to have access to psychological services, in time they will be able to move beyond the intense emotions that are associated with the grief of suicide.

A common statement repeatedly heard is how disappointed the family is with the department after the funeral. The support that may have been shown dissipates and the family is left feeling abandoned and isolated. Many of them need to know that the officer's peers are missing their loved one. They need to hear the stories of how their loved one helped, befriended, and even joked with them over the years. They need to know that their loved one's life mattered outside of their own family.

The key element to surviving a loss due to suicide is hope. Without hope of surviving this enormous pain, the survivors will be left with the same sense of despair as the person who took his or her own life.

Hope allows you to take your next breath, get out of bed, go to work, and raise your children. Without hope, there can be no tomorrow.

When a police officer dies by suicide, chaos and distress will inevitably occur, but departments can minimize errors by knowing how to respond to survivors (Tate, 2003).

Immediate Response

1. Police personnel making notification should arrive in unmarked cars.
2. Include the police chaplain or crisis counselor when making notification to the family.
3. An ambulance should be parked several blocks from the site of notification.
4. Ask the survivor who should be contacted for emotional support (i.e., a family member, a neighbor, or a friend).
5. Do not speculate or provide information that has not been confirmed.
6. Advise the family what will be said at the press conference, if one will be given.
7. Notify all police personnel that speaking to the media, even on condition of anonymity, is prohibited.
8. Assign a police officer or police chaplain to act as the liaison between the department and the family.

Within 48 Hours

1. The liaison officer has notified the department of the funeral arrangements.
2. Notification of funeral arrangement is provided to other jurisdictions, as well as city council, mayor's office, and so on.
3. Arrangements should be made with the other police jurisdictions to provide patrol support so that police officers, dispatchers, and other personnel may attend the funeral.
4. A benefits package (i.e., life insurance, health insurance, annuities) should be presented to the family by a qualified personnel employee.
5. Photocopy and return a copy of the suicide note to the family.

REFERENCES

Public Safety Officers' Benefits. Available: http://www.ojp.usdoj.gov/BJA/grant/psob/psob_main.html. March, 2010.

Tate, T. (2003). Police suicides: Responding to the needs of the family. In D. Hackett and J. M. Violanti (Eds.). *Police Suicide: Tactics for Prevention* (p. 118). Springfield, IL: Charles C Thomas.

Wikipedia (2010). Florida Mental Health Act. Available: http://en.wikipedia.org/wiki/Florida_Mental_Health_Act. Accessed May 3, 2010.

Chapter 8

WHAT NEXT? PREVENTION EFFORTS

ANDREW F. O'HARA, TERESA T. TATE, and JOHN M. VIOLANTI

AVOIDING THE EDGE – THE OTHER HALF OF THE EQUATION

Andrew F. O'Hara

Suicide prevention programs have saved police lives. Unfortunately, we continue to see a increase in lives lost to suicide. This is because we are limiting ourselves to only one half of the solution. There must be two parts:

- Career ESC training
- Effective suicide prevention programs

We must have suicide prevention as a response to those officers who are "on the edge." Relying on this alone, however, will never be enough to meet its goal. The numbers will continue to rise.

The only way we can round out the picture is to balance the appropriately reactive program (suicide prevention) with a proactive side to keep officers from ever getting that far in the first place. That role is fulfilled by the ESC program, which places officers in control of their own emotional well-being. We do not do it for them. The key is that we are putting them in charge – we are empowering them by providing them with the annual training, resources, and support to achieve their goals. We are, for the first time, placing their mental health on an equal footing with their physical health. ESC is a fitness program. In the same way that running and swimming are forms of physical fitness, ESC is mental fitness. It provides officers with the means by which they can avoid *getting* into trouble or *becoming* suicidal. It is possible to be both physically and emotionally fit throughout one's law enforcement career.

The possibilities are endless and exciting. Far too many officers are out there, below our radar, working and suffering from the caustic, hostile, embittering world they face, year after year and decade after decade. Through the overlapping of ESC and suicide prevention, we have a chance to change that. We will be preventing suicides, and much more. We will be inviting officers to take control of their mental health, take advantage of the training and resources we give them, and make healthy choices for themselves – freely and voluntarily. We do not expect miracles, but we cannot deny them the chance to enjoy good health!

It will begin slowly, but it will grow. We have a responsibility to our officers today and the future generations coming into law enforcement – to show them better ways than were shown us. This is our challenge to work together and create something that will make a difference. It needs doing.

If not now, when? If not us, who?

ON THE PATH TO PREVENTION

Teresa T. Tate

There has been a slow shift in the attitude of police administrators in understanding the complexity of why an officer takes his or her own life. The reasons are vast and are generally not due to just one circumstance but the buildup of different events in their lives.

Police departments, as well as training academies, are realizing the essential need in developing suicide awareness training. Implementing suicide awareness training as part of the academy curriculum provides new recruits an opportunity to erase the stigma associated with mental illness and suicide. By understanding the dynamics of the potential stress of a law enforcement career, these recruits will rise through the ranks with leadership skills that can benefit officers requiring psychological assistance before the crisis has reached a critical level.

Police officers and survivors were asked if $1 million were made available for law enforcement programs, how would they direct the money? The responses varied from annual mental health checkups through EAP services or an outside resource to funding for a national hotline specifically for law enforcement officers, mandate law enforcement agencies to report suicides of police officers for collection of data and statistics to one entity, and the creation and passage of a legislative bill outlining a criteria to classify specific cases of suicide as a line of duty death. Also mentioned and equally important was to mandate training within the police academies as well as in-service training.

Since 2001, Survivors of Law Enforcement Suicide (SOLES); the Florida Regional Community Policing Institute at St. Petersburg College; and the United States Attorney's Office, Middle District of Florida, have partnered together in offering a series of training seminars called, In Harm's Way: Tactics for Psychological Survival in Law Enforcement (IHW).

In 2005, Florida Governor Jeb Bush funded a statewide public service announcement (PSA) campaign for law enforcement suicide prevention. It was not until 2007 that the Florida statewide conference was held where more than 250 law enforcement personnel were in attendance. The development of the IHW Toolkit, complete with a resource CD and "Rolling Back-Up" CD with roll call and in-service videos were provided free to every law enforcement agency in Florida. Since that time, this partnership has assisted the Kansas, Missouri, California, and New Jersey U.S. Attorneys' Offices in offering IHW seminars. The IHW Toolkit was designed with input from law enforcement officers, as well as subject-matter experts, to help reduce the stigma associated with seeking help.

In 2008, the U.S. Department of Justice, Bureau of Justice Assistance funded a national IHW initiative for 2009. Information on this training initiative, as well as support programs for officers, is available on the Florida Regional Community Policing Institute (RCPI) web page at http://policesuicide.spcollege.edu. These resources were developed so that police departments could personalize the information utilizing their own agency logo as well as providing EAP, peer support, and chaplaincy contact information. The information can be used to present academy and in-service Law Enforcement Suicide Prevention Awareness Training, as well as to develop programs within their agency. Through this training and utilization of the IHW toolkit, agencies can implement programs to help officers continue their careers and reduce the risk that suicide may become a reality.

At the beginning of President Obama's term in 2009, Congress passed a $787 billion economic stimulus plan called the American Recovery and Reinvestment Act of 2009. In that bill, $4 billion were provided for law enforcement grants with an emphasis on job creation and job retention. Of the $4 billion, half was available through the Edward Byrne Memorial Justice Assistance Grant (JAG). The JAG funds may be used for state and local initiatives, technical assistance, training (including prevention and education programs), personnel equipment, supplies, contractual support, and information systems for criminal justice. Although law enforcement officers are always in need of better equipment and continuous training to protect and serve our communities, just how much of that stimulus money would be directed toward protecting the emotional well-being of police officers? It comes as a disappointment that in a preliminary search, no law enforcement agencies are utilizing these funds for law enforcement suicide prevention training. In fact, the Florida Department of Law Enforcement, the agency that oversees the dissemination of these funds in Florida, did not receive any applications from a law enforcement agency requesting funding on this issue.

The Bureau of Justice Assistance (BJA), which oversees the JAG program, allows agencies four years to utilize the funding. Even if a law enforcement agency requested funding for a certain program, the agency has the ability to redirect the funds to another program, in other words suicide prevention training. Perhaps within this time frame, law enforcement agencies will be making a concerted effort to address the issue of mental well-being for their officers by implementing training programs with available resources. Survivors have found that participating in suicide prevention training, as well as survivor support programs, offers them a chance to further their healing. It is an opportunity to turn a tragedy into a positive message. This is an outlet for survivors to eliminate the stigma associated with suicide and to remind others that we should be remembering officers for how they lived their life, not by how they died. Although survivors have expressed an interest in participating in such programs, the stigma continues to prevent many of them from discussing it in a public forum.

The emotional toll on a survivor who stands before a room of law enforcement officers, whether the audience is 10 or 250, can linger for weeks or months. The motivation for survivors to participate in suicide prevention training is the belief that every life matters and one suicide is too many. These survivors, whether they are spouses, parents, or other law enforcement officers, talk of a personal tragedy that many cannot even whisper about within their own families.

Police departments have a tendency to abandon or isolate the survivors immediately after the suicide or the funeral, depending on the circumstances. Survivors who request interaction with the officer's department are generally rebuffed. One rare exception can be noted. A mother who accompanied several officers from her son's department when they attended training on police suicide prevention was, in turn, provided the opportunity to present during training at her son's department. The mother spoke to his peers and offered insight into her son's life growing up as well as the devastating effects his suicide has had on her as well as his family. Many of the officers in attendance had worked with her son and felt comfortable talking to the mother. This opportunity not only provided education on suicide prevention but also allowed the officers a chance to express their feelings on the loss of their coworker and how much they continue to miss him. It is interesting to point out that survivors can find acceptance from law enforcement officers in other jurisdictions, even those jurisdictions that have lost officers to suicide, but not from their own "police family."

Cases involving an officer taking his or her own life within twenty-four to forty-eight hours after being placed on administrative leave with pay have left the surviving spouse feeling angry and betrayed by the police department. The circumstances of these cases generally involve alcohol abuse, prescription drug abuse, or behavioral changes due to depression or PTSD. Spouses are privy to information that administrators may not be aware of and want the officer to receive help without betraying the confidence of the officer or the repercussions that the officer may inflict upon them. Spouses also fear that the officer may lose his or her job instead of receiving help. Many widows are convinced that if only the department had advised them that their spouse was placed on administrative leave or had consulted them during the process of talking to the officer, they would have been able to intervene and perhaps prevent the suicide. In most marriages, the spouses feel protective toward their partner and believe that they may have control over the actions of that person.

Sheriff Kevin Rambosk, Collier County Sheriff's Office in Florida, has implemented a standard operating procedure (SOP) for situations involving deputies being placed on administrative leave with pay for various circumstances. These procedures do not apply to all cases; however, in the event of a deputy's being relieved of duty for alcohol abuse or mental health issues, the following is offered as guidance.

- The *option* is given to the deputy to bring his or her spouse to the initial meeting when the deputy will be told he or she will be on administrative leave with pay (not available in all cases).
- Administrators inform the deputy to tell the family to call if they have questions.
- The opportunity to set up a second meeting to explain the circumstances to the deputy's spouse is offered.
- The deputy has a mandatory appearance with the police psychologist immediately after notification of administrative leave.
- The deputy is taken by a member of the department's peer support team to the psychologist's office.
- The deputy receives paperwork of stress-related signs to take home.

In instances in which police officers end their life at the police station and possibly in front of their supervisors or peers, it is essential that all officers present be debriefed. No officer should be allowed to leave the station without the administration's knowing that a family member or friend will be at the home when the officer arrives. It is understandable that the department will put priority on the emotional well-being of these affected officers first, but at the same time, the department cannot forget the family of the officer who died. A police chaplain can be a valuable resource as a liaison between the family and the department. It is important that the department not withdraw from the officer's family while trying to help their own.

Police departments may also consider offering a family debriefing the following day. This will give the officers and their spouses an opportunity to share their feelings, as well as provide the spouses with information on the possible emotional effects the suicide may have on the officer as a survivor.

Whether the act occurs in front of the officer's supervisors or peers or whether it occurs at a public park or road, each officer who witnessed the act or found the deceased officer needs to be debriefed. In addition to the debriefing, the opportunity to seek counseling services to deal with any intrusive thoughts, nightmares, or behavioral changes should be a supportive and private option for the police officers.

The prevailing question of how many more officers must die by their own hand before action is taken to prevent this tragedy from happening – repeatedly in some departments – continues. We must never forget that suicide is a national health concern. Suicide does not discriminate based on race, gender, age, social background, religious belief, or profession. Many cases of suicide can be prevented, but without awareness and educational training on the issue of suicide, this silent epidemic within law enforcement agencies will continue.

MOVING ON: BACK FROM THE EDGE

John M. Violanti

As mentioned in Chapter One, we are faced with many challenges in police suicide prevention efforts. Those challenges remain steadfast in the path of successful prevention. We have not yet learned the prevalence and incidence of suicide in law enforcement. We only know that, in most cases, the rate is higher than in other working or general populations. The obvious solution is to conduct further and more careful research on a wider scale. Working on denial by police departments that suicide is a problem is no easy task. It appears, however, through the efforts of groups such as Badge of Life (BOL) and SOLES that police agencies are beginning to understand the seriousness of suicide risk in police work. There is also a lack of sufficient information as to why police suicide occurs, calling for a more in-depth research into the lives and experiences of those officers who do commit suicide.

What happens in a department after a suicide can be devastating. Quite often, entire departments succumb to a depressed mood and productivity falls. There is often a grief wave in the department when an officer suicides. Police administrators have commented that somehow their officers do not seem the same after a suicide; supervisors notice an effect on morale, happiness, and work. This emphasizes the need to recognize and prevent suicides among police personnel. "Postvention" involves a designed plan to help reduce the negative impact on departments and family. Postvention is essential because it allows for the proper grieving of survivors and departments and shows that someone cares enough to be concerned about those who survive suicide. Police leaders should arrange for psychological debriefings after the suicide of an officer that will help individual survivors and the department deal with the crisis.

One of the most distressing events in law enforcement is the suicide of an officer. For survivors, the sudden or unexpected death of a loved one can be a traumatic life event. Although most duty-related deaths are distressful, suicide may create even more trauma for survivors. It is unfortunate that survivors of police suicide must deal not only with their own grief but also with negative reactions of police peers, the organization, and the public. The police work group has the *potential* to provide a supportive set of conditions in reducing psychological distress, because it provides environmental structure, leadership, companionship, and a source of motivation for recovery. Quite often, however, survivors of police suicide are abandoned more quickly than those of officers who died from other causes. Police officials may not place much emphasis on assisting survivors of police suicide due to the stigma associated with such deaths. In her chapter, Teresa T. Tate, founder of SOLES, discussed how the police agency can better help survivors of suicide. The actions and reactions of the police chief down to the patrol officer will forever be remembered by a survivor. The trauma that survivors experience may vary from visual effects to improper notification, department speculation, and lack of compassion toward survivors. The survivors, as well as the police department, may embark on a painful journey for years to come.

Future Research Considerations

Psychological autopsies may be an important research tool in determining police suicide precedents. The issues of stress, PTSD, alcohol use, depression, and relationship problems must be further explored. This research design will allow us to examine risk factors reportedly associated with police suicide. Most previous studies on police suicide provide evidence of high risk but fall short in explaining precipitant individual and social factors involved in police suicide. This lack of information impedes efforts at suicide prevention among the police, other similar occupations, and specific age groups. In future work, we must employ a valid design. The "psychological autopsy" is well-established as the means for obtaining comprehensive retrospective information about victims of completed suicide.

Psychological Autopsy Hypotheses

The following are ideas about why police officers might decide to choose suicide:

- Police officers who commit suicide will more often have suffered from current active and lifetime diagnoses of major affective disorders, substance abuse disorders, and their comorbidity
- Police suicide victims will more likely to experienced severe violence at work in their lifetime
- Police officers who commit suicide will (1) have experienced more life event stressors; and (2) have smaller social networks, with which they interact less frequently, and which they derive less instrumental support
- Police officers who have a history of alcohol abuse are more likely to complete suicide
- Police officers have instant access to firearms which they use in work. We hypothesize that police officers will be more likely to complete suicide with a firearm than other methods
- Police officers are hesitant and untrusting when it comes to visiting health care professionals. No study has yet investigated whether police officers who go on to commit suicide are more or less likely to have asked for help from an EAP or mental health professional
- Police officers who commit suicide will be more likely to have been exposed to or involved in stressful traumatic events in their work (Hackett & Violanti, 2003).

The issues highlighted in this book deserve serious consideration in order to advance police suicide prevention. A number of medical, psychological, and social influences appear to be associated with police suicide, and knowledge of these influences is necessary in order to reach that goal. All too often we emphasize the dangers of police work but seem to neglect the hidden psychological danger of this profession. Suicide is a consequence of that hidden danger. It is a clear indication of the intolerable strain placed on the police officer's work and life roles. In the least, we should adequately address this problem and provide methods and means to prevent future tragedies, for fear that more officers may fall from the edge.

REFERENCES

Hackett, D., & Violanti, J. M. (Eds.) (2003). *Police suicide: Tactics for intervention* (p. 123). Springfield, IL: Charles C Thomas.

INDEX

ABOUT THE AUTHORS

John M. Violanti, Ph.D., is a research professor in the Department of Social and Preventive Medicine, School of Public Health and Health Professions at the State University of New York (SUNY) Buffalo, and a member of the SUNY at Buffalo School of Medicine graduate faculty. He is a police veteran, serving with the New York State Police for twenty-three years as a trooper, the Bureau of Criminal Investigation, and later as a coordinator of the Psychological Assistance Program for the State Police. He has been involved in the design, implementation, and analysis of numerous police-related stress and health studies over the past twenty years. Past projects include studies on police mortality, police stress and trauma, and suicide. His most recent work involves the collection of data on physiological stress and subclinical cardiovascular and metabolic consequences in police officers. Dr. Violanti has authored more than fifty peer-reviewed articles and has written and edited eleven books on topics of police stress, psychological trauma, and suicide. He has been an invited lecturer on police stress at the FBI Academy at Quantico, Virginia, several times. He has lectured nationally and internationally at academic institutions and police agencies on matters of suicide, stress, and trauma at work.

Andrew F. O'Hara is a military veteran and a twenty-four–year retiree of the California Highway Patrol. He retired as a sergeant, having spent the majority of his time on the streets, and ended his career with severe posttraumatic stress disorder and a near suicide. Following lengthy recovery, he went on to found the Badge of Life, a nonprofit organization that goes beyond mere suicide prevention to promote the career-long emotional well-being of police officers. As executive director of that organization, O'Hara writes and speaks internationally on the need for law enforcement to broaden its focus to the real needs of its personnel in the modern age. During 2008 and 2009, he joined Dr. John Violanti in a first of its kind study of annual police suicides in the United States, resulting in a definitive picture of what is occurring nationally, state by state and case by case, for future research and program development.

Teresa T. Tate became a survivor of suicide in 1989 and is an advocate for survivors of law enforcement suicide. In 1995, she is the founder of a national network called Survivors of Law Enforcement Suicide and offers assistance to law enforcement families as well as departments when a police officer suicide has occurred. While employed with the Bureau of Alcohol, Tobacco and Firearms (ATF), she was a member of ATF's peer support team and attended several critical incident/peer support training seminars. Ms. Tate has written articles on law enforcement suicide for various magazines, and newsletters and was a contributing writer to the book, *Police Suicide: Tactics for Prevention.* In February 1997, she was the first survivor to speak at a suicide awareness conference for police officers, which was sponsored by the Fraternal Order of Police. Since 2001, she has partnered with several law enforcement organizations in developing and presenting a nationwide training program for police officers called In Harm's Way. Ms. Tate also addresses the issue of survivor support in her community and is credited for the development and implementation of the Survivor of Suicide support group in Lee County, Florida.